SPECTRUM®

Test Prep

Grade 7

Published by Spectrum®
an imprint of Carson-Dellosa Publishing LLC
Greensboro, NC

Visit *carsondellosa.com* for correlations to Common Core State, national and Canadian provincial standards.

Spectrum®
An imprint of Carson-Dellosa Publishing LLC
P.O. Box 35665
Greensboro, NC 27425 USA

ISBN 0-7696-8627-3

11-118147784

Table of Contents

Social Studies

Science

What's Inside?

This workbook is designed to help you and your seventh grader understand what he or she will be expected to know on standardized tests.

Practice Pages

The workbook is divided into four sections: English Language Arts, Mathematics, Social Studies, and Science. The practice activities in this workbook provide students with practice in each of these areas. Each section has practice activities that have questions similar to those that will appear on the standardized tests. Students should use a pencil to fill in the correct answers and to complete any writing on these activities.

National Standards

Before each practice section is a list of the national standards covered by that section. These standards list the knowledge and skills that students are expected to master at each grade level. The shaded *What it means* sections will help to explain any information in the standards that might be unfamiliar.

Mini-Tests and Final Tests

When your student finishes the practice pages for specific standards, he or she can move on to a mini-test that covers the material presented on those practice activities. After an entire set of standards and accompanying practice pages are completed, your student should take the final test, which incorporates materials from all the practice pages in that section.

Final Test Answer Sheet

The final tests have a separate answer sheet that mimics the style of the answer sheets the students will use on the standardized tests. The answer sheets appear at the end of each final test.

How Am I Doing?

The *How Am I Doing?* pages are designed to help students identify areas where they are proficient and areas where they still need more practice. They will pinpoint areas where more work is needed as well as areas where your student excels. Students can keep track of each of their mini-test scores on these pages.

Answer Key

Answers to all the practice pages, mini-tests, and final tests are listed by page number and appear at the end of the book.

To find a complete listing of the national standards in each subject area, you can access the following Web sites:

The National Council of Teachers of English: www.ncte.org
National Council of Teachers of Mathematics: www.nctm.org/standards
National Council for the Social Studies: www.ncss.org/standards
National Science Teachers Association: www.nsta.org/standards

English Language Arts Standards

Standard 1 *(See pages 9–12.)*
Students read a wide range of print and nonprint texts to build an understanding of texts, of themselves, and of the cultures of the United States and the world; to acquire new information; to respond to the needs and demands of society and the workplace; and for personal fulfillment. Among these texts are fiction and nonfiction, classic and contemporary works.

Standard 2 *(See pages 11–14.)*
Students read a wide range of literature from many periods in many genres to build an understanding of the many dimensions (e.g., philosophical, ethical, aesthetic) of human experience.

Standard 3 *(See pages 15–17.)*
Students apply a wide range of strategies to comprehend, interpret, evaluate, and appreciate texts. They draw on their prior experience, their interactions with other readers and writers, their knowledge of word meaning and of other texts, their word identification strategies, and their understanding of textual features (e.g., sound-letter correspondence, sentence structure, context, graphics).

Standard 4 *(See pages 19–21.)*
Students adjust their use of spoken, written, and visual language (e.g., conventions, style, vocabulary) to communicate effectively with a variety of audiences and for different purposes.

Standard 5 *(See pages 22–24.)*
Students employ a wide range of strategies as they write and use different writing process elements appropriately to communicate with different audiences for a variety of purposes.

Standard 6 *(See pages 25–28.)*
Students apply knowledge of language structure, language conventions (e.g., spelling and punctuation), media techniques, figurative language, and genre to create, critique, and discuss print and nonprint texts.

Standard 7 *(See pages 30–31.)*
Students conduct research on issues and interests by generating ideas and questions, and by posing problems. They gather, evaluate, and synthesize data from a variety of sources (e.g., print and nonprint texts, artifacts, people) to communicate their discoveries in ways that suit their purpose and audience.

Standard 8 *(See page 32.)*
Students use a variety of technological and informational resources (e.g., libraries, databases, computer networks, video) to gather and synthesize information and to create and communicate knowledge.

Standard 9 *(See page 34.)*
Students develop an understanding of and respect for diversity in language use, patterns, and dialects across cultures, ethnic groups, geographic regions, and social roles.

English Language Arts Standards

Standard 10
Students whose first language is not English make use of their first language to develop competency in the English language arts and to develop understanding of content across the curriculum.

Standard 11 *(See page 35.)*
Students participate as knowledgeable, reflective, creative, and critical members of a variety of literacy communities.

Standard 12 *(See page 36.)*
Students use spoken, written, and visual language to accomplish their own purposes (e.g., for learning, enjoyment, persuasion, and the exchange of information).

Name _____ Date _____

1.0

Reading to Acquire Information
Reading and Comprehension

DIRECTIONS: Read the passage, and then answer the questions on the next page.

 Read the questions first. Think about them as you read the passage.

From Dreams to Reality

People have probably always dreamed of flight. As they watched birds fly, they wished that they could soar into the blue sky. As they watched the night sky, they wished they could explore the distant bright specks called *stars*. These dreams led inventors and scientists to risk their lives to achieve flight.

Orville and Wilbur Wright's first flight at Kitty Hawk in 1903 was only the beginning. Flight continued to improve and dreams soared further into space. The first manned space flight occurred in 1961 when Russian cosmonaut Yuri A. Gagarin orbited Earth a single time. In 1963, the first woman cosmonaut, Valentina Tereshkova, orbited the Earth 48 times.

The Russians led the space race for many years. In 1965, another cosmonaut, Alesksei A. Leonov, took the first space walk. In 1968, the Russians launched an unmanned spacecraft that orbited the Moon. The pictures that returned to Earth encouraged man to take the next step to land on the Moon.

The United States became the leader in the space race when *Apollo 11* landed on the Moon in 1969. Neil Armstrong was the first man to step on the lunar surface. As he did so, he said these famous words, "That's one small step for a man, one giant leap for mankind." Later in 1969, Charles Conrad, Jr. and Alan L. Bean returned to the Moon. In 1972, the United States completed its last mission to the Moon with the launch of *Apollo 17.*

Today, people continue their quest for space, gathering data from the International Space Station. In addition, unmanned probes have flown deep into space toward the planets, sending back pictures and scientific readings.

GO

1. **What is this passage mainly about?**

    (A)   famous cosmonauts

    (B)   a brief history of human flight

    (C)   the first flight

    (D)   the space race

2. **What happened first?**

    (F)   The International Space Station was launched.

    (G)   Yuri Gagarin orbited Earth a single time.

    (H)   Neil Armstrong walked on the Moon.

    (J)   The first woman orbited Earth.

3. **Why do you suppose the race to achieve firsts in space travel was so important?**

    (A)   It prompted the United States to excel in space exploration.

    (B)   It encouraged cooperation between the two countries.

    (C)   It discouraged people from being interested in space travel.

    (D)   It developed fierce rivalry that led to many mistakes.

4. **Which of these is an opinion?**

    (F)   The United States became the leader in the space race with the first landing on the Moon.

    (G)   All people have dreamed about being able to fly.

    (H)   Today, unmanned space probes explore space.

    (J)   The Russians led the space race for several years.

5. **What is the purpose of this passage?**

    (A)   to inform

    (B)   to advertise

    (C)   to entertain

    (D)   to promote an idea

6. **Which statement is false?**

    (F)   The first woman in space was Valentina Tereshkova.

    (G)   The first landing on the Moon was in 1969.

    (H)   Russia achieved the first manned space flight.

    (J)   The last landing on the Moon in 1972 ended the space race.

7. **Who was the first man to step on the moon?**

    (A)   Yuri Gagarin

    (B)   Orville Wright

    (C)   Neil Armstrong

    (D)   Alan Bean

8. *Apollo 11* **was the name of _____ .**

    (F)   Orville and Wilbur Wright's first airplane

    (G)   the first manned space flight

    (H)   the first American space mission to the Moon

    (J)   the last American space mission to the Moon

9. **Which of the following can not be determined from the passage?**

    (A)   the first words spoken on the Moon

    (B)   the cost of the American space program

    (C)   the location of Orville and Wilbur Wright's first flight

    (D)   the year the United States became the leader in the space race

10. **Which statement is supported by the passage?**

    (F)   Alesksei A. Leonov is the most famous cosmonaut.

    (G)   Cosmonauts and astronauts were brave and adventurous.

    (H)   Americans are better scientists than Russians.

    (J)   Many people were interested in space exploration in the 1960s and 1970s, but few people are interested in it today.

Responding to Fiction
Reading and Comprehension

The Escape

Into the shady glen the small figure rode on a pony little larger than a dog. The pony's breath misted in the crisp air as the beast blew air out of its nostrils. The green-mantled figure patted the neck of the beast, whispering words of comfort into the animal's ear. In response, the faithful steed nickered, thumped his wide hoofs twice upon the soft bed of the forest floor, and ceased its shaking.

"We've left the raiders behind, old friend," said Rowan, as she removed her hooded mantle and tossed her head back and forth, bringing peace to her own troubled mind. Rowan was one of four daughters of Sylvia, guide of all wood folk.

Suddenly, shouts of rough men cut through the glade's peace.

"In here, I tell ya. The maid's gone to hiding in this grove."

"Nah, ya lunk. She'd never wait for us here. Not after she dunked old Stefan at the marsh. No! She's a gone on to her crazy folk, don'tcha know."

The two gray-cloaked riders dismounted, still arguing as they examined the earth for traces of the child's flight.

"Who was the lout who let her escape?" asked the first.

"'Tis one who no longer breathes the air so freely," returned the second grimly. "The lord nearly choked the fool, even as the knave begged for mercy. Ah, there's little patience for one who lets a mystic escape, to be true!"

Five nobly dressed horsemen wove through the trees to the clearing where these two rustics still squatted. In the lead came the fierce lord, a huge form with scarlet and gray finery worn over his coat of mail.

"What say you?" he roared. "Have you found the trail of Rowan?"

"No, sire," spoke the first gray, trembling, "though I was certain the child headed into this wood. Shall I continue to search, lord?"

"Aye, indeed," replied the master calmly, controlled. "She is here. I know it, too. You have a keen sense for the hunt, Mikkel. Be at ready with your blade. And you too, Short Brush! Though a child, our Rowan is vicious with her weapon."

"Yes, sire," agreed Mikkel and Short Brush.

The two grays beat the bushes in the search. Closer and closer they came to the child's hiding place, a small earthen scoop created when the roots of a wind-blown tree pulled free of the earth.

The evil lord and his lot remained mounted, ready to pursue should the young girl determine to take flight once more. And so, they were not prepared for the child's play.

Rowan softly, softly sang, "You wind-whipped branches shudder, shake. You oaks and cedars, tremble. Take these men and beasts who do us wrong. Not in these woods do they belong."

As a mighty gust of wind roared, nearby trees slapped their branches to the point of breaking, reaching out and grasping the five mounted men. An immense gaping cavern opened in the trunk of an ancient oak and swallowed the five surprised mail-clad men whole.

Mikkel and Short Brush, too, were lifted high into the air by a white pine and a blue spruce. Lifted high. Kept high. For a while.

"Return from whence you came. Go to your families, and tell them of the wrath of Sylvia," commanded Rowan. "She would not wish you to come to her land again!"

The pine and spruce tossed the two gray trackers over the trees of the forest and into the field beyond. The field was already harvested and soggy with the rains of autumn. Mikkel and Short Brush, unhurt but shaken by their arboreal flight, rose and fled immediately to tell their master of the strange doings of this wood.

GO →

DIRECTIONS: Read the story on the previous page, and then answer the questions.

1. **What details tell the reader that Rowan is very small?**

   _____

   _____

   _____

   _____

   _____

2. **What details help you picture the fierce lord?**

   _____

   _____

   _____

   _____

   _____

3. **What details convey that Rowan is in great danger if caught?**

   _____

   _____

   _____

   _____

   _____

4. **To which genre does this story belong?**

   (F) science fiction

   (G) mystery

   (H) fantasy/adventure

   (J) satire

5. **Which statement about Rowan is supported by the text?**

   (A) She has magical powers.

   (B) She has a vivid imagination.

   (C) She is the greatest beauty in the land.

   (D) She wishes one day to become queen.

6. **From reading the story, we can conclude that** _____ .

   (F) the horsemen chasing Rowan are cowards

   (G) whoever captures Rowan will become a mystic

   (H) the horsemen hope to kidnap Rowan and hold her for ransom

   (J) Rowan will fiercely defend the woods she loves

STOP

English Language Arts

| 2.0 |

Understanding and Using Literary Terms
Reading and Comprehension

DIRECTIONS: Read the poem.

The Little Black-Eyed Rebel

A poem by Will Carleton

A boy drove into the city, his wagon
    loaded down
With food to feed the people of the
    British-governed town;
And the little black-eyed rebel, so
    innocent and sly,
Was watching for his coming from the
    corner of her eye. . . .

He drove up to the market, he waited in
    the line;
His apples and potatoes were fresh and
    fair and fine;
But long and long he waited, and no one
    came to buy,
Save the black-eyed rebel, watching
    from the corner of her eye.

"Now who will buy my apples?" he
    shouted, long and loud;
And "Who wants my potatoes?" he
    repeated to the crowd;
But from all the people round him came
    no word of reply,
Save the black-eyed rebel, answering
    from the corner of her eye.

For she knew that 'neath the lining of the
    coat he wore that day,
Were long letters from the husbands and
    the fathers far away,
Who were fighting for the freedom that
    they meant to gain or die;
And a tear like silver glistened in the
    corner of her eye.

But the treasures—how to get them?
    crept the questions through her
    mind,
Since keen enemies were watching for
    what prizes they might find;
And she paused a while and pondered,
    with a pretty little sigh;
Then resolve crept through her features,
    and a shrewdness fired her eye.

So she resolutely walked up to the
    wagon old and red;
"May I have a dozen apples for a kiss?"
    she sweetly said:
And the brown face flushed to scarlet;
    for the boy was somewhat shy,
And he saw her laughing at him from the
    corner of her eye. . . .

Clinging round his brawny neck, she
    clasped her fingers white and small,
And then whispered, "Quick! the letters!
    thrust them underneath my shawl!
Carry back again this package, and be
    sure that you are spry!"
And she sweetly smiled upon him from
    the corner of her eye. . . .

With the news of loved ones absent to
    the dear friends they would greet,
Searching them who hungered for them,
    swift she glided through the street.
"There is nothing worth the doing
    that it does not pay to try,"
Thought the little black-eyed rebel,
    with a twinkle in her eye.

GO

Name _____ Date _____

DIRECTIONS: Several literary terms are listed below. Identify and describe them using the poem on page 13.

The heroine's name was Mary Redmond, and she lived in Philadelphia. During the occupation of that town by the British, she was ever ready to aid in the secret delivery of the letters written home by the husbands and fathers fighting in the Continental Army.

Setting _____

_____

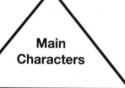

Main Characters _____

_____

Plot

Problem: _____

_____

Goal: _____

_____

Episodes _____

_____

Climax _____

_____

Resolution _____

_____

STOP

English Language Arts

[3.0]

Analyzing Unfamiliar Vocabulary
Reading and Comprehension

DIRECTIONS: Read the poem, and answer the questions that follow.

Bishop Loreless

Bishop loreless,°
King redeless,°
Young men reckless,°
Old man witless
Woman shameless—
    I swear by heaven's king
    Those be five lither thing!

°*lore*—learning, knowledge
°*redeless*—without advice or guidance
°*reckless*—heedless

"Bishop Loreless" is an English poem that was written more than 600 years ago. The English language has changed quite a bit since then. Even though this poem is written in English, you are probably not familiar with some of the words. Use the mini-dictionary that accompanies the poem to help your understanding.

1. **According to the poet, it is important for all kings to have _____ .**
   - (A) extensive landholdings
   - (B) wise advisors or counselors
   - (C) great wealth
   - (D) experience in battle

2. **The best definition of the word *loreless* is _____ .**
   - (F) knowledgeable
   - (G) irresponsible
   - (H) ignorant
   - (J) wicked

3. **According to the poet, it is bad for which group to be irresponsible?**
   - (A) bishops
   - (B) women
   - (C) old men
   - (D) young men

4. **A definition for the phrase *lither thing* is not provided for you. Based on the rest of the poem, what do you think the phrase means?**
   - (F) respectable things
   - (G) beautiful things
   - (H) evil things
   - (J) happy things

STOP

3.0

Identifying Main Ideas
and Supporting Elements
Reading and Comprehension

DIRECTIONS: Read the passage, and then answer the questions on the next page.

Yellowstone

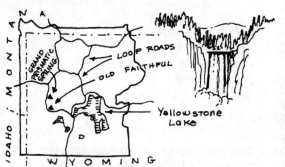

Yellowstone National Park is the site of some of the most famous natural wonders in the world, including geysers, hot springs, deep canyons, waterfalls, and great evergreen forests. Yellowstone is the oldest national park in the United States. It covers an area of land approximately 60 by 50 miles. Most of the land is located in the state of Wyoming, but it also spreads into Idaho and Montana. Scientists believe that the landscape of Yellowstone was created by a series of volcanic eruptions thousands of years ago. Molten rock, called *magma,* remains under the park. The heat from the magma produces the 200 geysers and thousands of hot springs for which Yellowstone is well-known.

Of all the wonders in Yellowstone, the main attraction is a famous geyser, Old Faithful. Approximately every 65 minutes, Old Faithful erupts for three to five minutes. The geyser erupts in a burst of boiling water that jumps 100 feet in the air. Other geysers in the park produce a spectacular sight, but none are as popular as Old Faithful.

Geysers may differ in frequency of eruption and size, but they all work in much the same way. As water seeps into the ground, it collects around the hot magma. The heated water produces steam, which rises and pushes up the cooler water above it. When the pressure becomes too great, the water erupts into the air. The cooled water falls back to the ground, and the cycle begins again.

The magma under the park also produces bubbling hot springs and mud pools, called *mudpots.* The largest hot spring in Yellowstone is Grand Prismatic Spring. It measures 370 feet wide.

Yellowstone Lake measures over 20 miles long and 14 miles wide. It is the largest high-altitude lake in North America. It lies almost 8,000 feet above sea level.

Evergreen forests of pine, fir, and spruce trees cover 90 percent of Yellowstone Park. Two hundred species of birds are found in Yellowstone. More than 40 kinds of other animals live in Yellowstone, which is the largest wildlife preserve in the United States. Visitors to the park may see bears, bison, cougars, moose, and mule deer.

Yellowstone National Park offers more than 1,000 miles of hiking trails. Over 2 million people visit the park each year.

GO →

1. **Choose the title that best reflects the main idea of this passage.**

   Ⓐ "Yellowstone's High-Altitude Lake"

   Ⓑ "An Amazing Wildlife Preserve"

   Ⓒ "Old Faithful Still Faithful"

   Ⓓ "The Natural Wonders of Yellowstone"

2. **Which of the following statements is not true?**

   Ⓕ Old Faithful erupts for a period of three to five minutes.

   Ⓖ Geysers differ in size, and they all work in very different ways.

   Ⓗ After a geyser erupts, the cooled water falls back to the ground.

   Ⓙ The boiling water of Old Faithful jumps 100 feet in the air.

3. **Most of Yellowstone National Park is located in the state of _____ .**

   Ⓐ California

   Ⓑ Idaho

   Ⓒ Wyoming

   Ⓓ Utah

4. **Which of the following is not a natural wonder found at Yellowstone?**

   Ⓕ volcanoes

   Ⓖ waterfalls

   Ⓗ hot springs

   Ⓙ geysers

DIRECTIONS: Fill in the web below based on information in the passage. Include two supporting details for each natural wonder.

5.

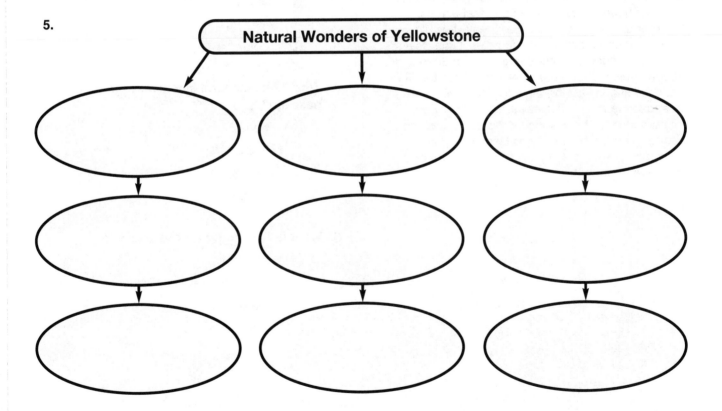

STOP

English Language Arts

1.0–3.0

For pages 9–17

Mini-Test 1

Reading and Comprehension

DIRECTIONS: Read the story below, and then answer the questions that follow.

A New Tepee

Fingers of frost tickled Little Deer's feet. It was a chilly fall morning, but there was no time for Little Deer to snuggle beneath her buffalo skins. It was going to be a busy day, helping her mother to finish the cover for their family's new tepee.

Little Deer slid her tunic over her head and fastened her moccasins. Wrapping herself up in another skin, she walked outside to survey the work they had done so far. The tepee cover was beautiful and nearly complete. The vast semicircle was spread across the ground, a patchwork in various shades of brown. After her father and brothers had killed the buffalo, she and her mother had carefully cured and prepared the skins, stretching them and scraping them until they were buttery soft. Then, with needles made from bone and thread made from animal sinew, they had carefully sewn the hides together until they formed a huge canvas nearly thirty feet across.

After they finished the cover today, it would be ready to mount on the lodge poles. Little Deer's father had traded with another tribe for fourteen tall, wooden poles. They would stack the poles together in a cone shape, lashing them together with more rope made from animal sinews. Then, they would carefully stretch the cover over the poles, forming a snug, watertight home. Little Deer smiled in anticipation. She could just imagine the cozy glow of the fire through the tepee walls at night.

1. **What is this story mainly about?**
   - Ⓐ hunting
   - Ⓑ building a tepee
   - Ⓒ the uses of buffalo
   - Ⓓ the life of a Native American girl

2. **To what genre does this passage belong?**
   - Ⓕ fiction
   - Ⓖ poetry
   - Ⓗ nonfiction
   - Ⓙ fable

3. **How does Little Deer feel about finishing the tepee?**
   - Ⓐ depressed
   - Ⓑ angry
   - Ⓒ excited
   - Ⓓ cold

4. **What does the term *sinew* mean in this passage?**
   - Ⓕ bone
   - Ⓖ wood
   - Ⓗ tendon
   - Ⓙ patchwork

5. **What is the setting for this passage?**
   - Ⓐ a campfire
   - Ⓑ a Native American village
   - Ⓒ the prairie
   - Ⓓ the woods

STOP

English Language Arts

| 4.0 |

Types of Pronouns
Writing

DIRECTIONS: In the sentences below, tell which type of pronoun is indicated in italics.

> A **pronoun** is used in place of a noun to refer to the person, place, or thing the noun names. Here are some common types of pronouns.
>
> **Personal pronouns** refer to a person or persons. For example, *I, you, he, she, it, we, they, them.*
>
> **Possessive pronouns** show that something belongs to someone. For example, *mine, hers, its, yours.*
>
> **Interrogative pronouns** are used in questions. For example, *who, what, which.*
>
> **Demonstrative pronouns** point out a specific person or thing. For example, *this, that, such, these, those.*
>
> **Reflexive pronouns** refer back to a noun or pronoun used earlier. For example, *itself, ourselves, myself, yourself.*
>
> **Indefinite pronouns** refer to other people or things in general, not specifically. For example, *any, someone, nothing, everybody.*

_____ 1. I want to tell *you* a secret.

_____ 2. *Everybody* knows that Tariq is the smartest one in class.

_____ 3. Ben wants *this* piece of cake for dessert.

_____ 4. Taylor can go to the park *herself.*

_____ 5. My car is in the repair shop, so we'll have to take *yours* to the mall.

_____ 6. Jerri tried to reason with *them,* but it was no use.

_____ 7. If *she* thinks I'm going to clean up this mess, she's badly mistaken!

_____ 8. *Who* did you invite to the party?

_____ 9. I think *we* all know what we must do.

_____ 10. *Those* belong to Barry, I think.

_____ 11. *What* is crawling up my arm?

_____ 12. When Alice saw the puppy, *she* began to laugh with joy.

_____ 13. The candy is *mine,* but I'll let you have some.

STOP

Name _____ Date _____

4.0

Adjectives, Adverbs, and Prepositional Phrases
Writing

DIRECTIONS: Underline each prepositional phrase in the sentences below.

1. **The watch was still in the box.**

2. **The children's artwork is displayed at city hall.**

3. **The cat's food dish is under the bag.**

4. **Last Friday was the due date for the library book.**

5. **The singer bowed to the applause of the crowd.**

DIRECTIONS: Add a prepositional phrase to each sentence and rewrite it on the lines provided.

6. **Mike called yesterday.**

   _____

   _____

7. **Kim searched the garage.**

   _____

   _____

8. **Lisa stopped the car.**

   _____

   _____

9. **Kira looked puzzled.**

   _____

   _____

DIRECTIONS: Write whether the word in bold type is an adjective or an adverb.

10. **both** puppies_____

11. **blue** sky_____

12. ran **quickly** _____

13. **bad** report _____

14. finish **easily** _____

15. **soft** blanket _____

DIRECTIONS: Write a paragraph describing your favorite place in the world. Circle each adjective and adverb you use in your description.

16. _____

   _____

   _____

   _____

   _____

   _____

   _____

   _____

   _____

   _____

   _____

STOP

English Language Arts

4.0

Using Verbs
Writing

DIRECTIONS: Underline the action verbs and circle the linking verbs in the sentences below.

> **Action verbs** show action or something that is happening. Example: We flew to New York. The action verb is *flew*.
>
> **Linking verbs** connect, or link, the subject with one or more words in the predicate that tell something about the subject. Some common linking verbs are *is, am, are, do, did, be, been, being, becomes, was*, and *were*.
>
> **Helping verbs** help the main verb. They come before the main verb. Some common helping verbs are *have, has, had, is, are, was, were, shall, will, be, been, do, did, does, may*, and *might*.

1. The day was warm and sunny.

2. The Nettler children were ready for the beach.

3. The children lived in San Diego.

4. They grabbed their beach towels and headed for the jeep.

5. On the way, they stopped for sandwiches.

6. Mary was the first to hit the sand.

7. Helen appears to be the practical daughter.

8. She found a table for their lunch.

9. John and Tom became the carriers of the surfboards.

10. All four teenagers rode the waves before lunch.

11. Tom crashed into the waves often.

DIRECTIONS: Underline the main verb and circle the helping verb in the sentences below.

12. The weather is turning cooler.

13. The holidays will be coming soon.

14. Chris is getting her house ready for the family.

15. Patrick and Michael might look for a tree tonight.

16. Kerry said, "I will make the cookies."

17. "You should go to the store first," said Chris.

18. You may help me if you like.

19. They had been working in the kitchen most of the day.

20. Michael could drive the tree home in his pickup truck.

21. This should be a wonderful family celebration.

Name _____   Date _____

English Language Arts

Writing with Organization
Writing

DIRECTIONS: Write a composition on the following subject: How has the world changed because of cellular phones?

_____

_____

_____

_____

_____

_____

_____

_____

_____

_____

_____

_____

_____

_____

_____

_____

_____

_____

DIRECTIONS: Review your composition. Use the following checklist to help you evaluate the organization of the composition.

Does the composition have an introduction, a body, and a conclusion?

_____

Is the topic clearly stated?

_____

Is there a logical order between sentences?

_____

Does the composition have at least three examples of the effects of cellular phone use on society?

_____

If necessary, reorganize your composition to include the items in the checklist.

Name _____ Date _____

Impact of Word Choice on Content
Writing

DIRECTIONS: In the story, several different words are used in place of *ran* and *screamed*. Find and list them below.

Score!

It was one of the closest games of the season. The teams were so evenly matched that neither team had been able to score. Time was running out. No score would mean overtime, but one good kick could mean winning the game.

Justin dashed down the soccer field toward the goal. "I'm open!" he shouted. "Pass the ball." He scanned the field around him, searching for a player from his team. "Brian, over here!"

Brian kicked the ball toward Justin, but before Justin could reach it, one of the opponents darted in and booted the ball away.

"Don't worry. We'll get it next time," yelled the coach as Brian sprinted back to regain possession of the ball.

This time, Brian dribbled out the wing, beating opponent after opponent. He centered the ball, and Justin bolted up just in time to kick it toward the goal. It was caught by the goalie. The goalie threw the ball back into play.

"Nice try! You almost had it!" shouted the coach as the team rushed back down the field.

The opponents now had possession of the ball. They flew past the first defender, took a shot at the goal, and missed.

"Make this one count!" bellowed the goalie as he kicked the ball out to his team.

Brian was determined to score. The game was nearly over, but there was still no score on the board. If either team could score a point before time was up, they would win the game. He raced down the field. He could hear the fans in the background. "Go! Score!" they roared.

In a last effort, the whole team charged down to help him out. They passed the ball around the opponents and worked closer and closer to the goal. Justin passed the ball to Brian, who took aim at the goal and gave it a mighty kick. The shot was good! The team had won!

"Congratulations! You guys were great! What a game! What a team!" cheered the fans.

Justin beamed with pride as he and the other players headed off the field.

1. ran:

_____

_____

_____

2. screamed:

_____

_____

_____

DIRECTIONS: In the space below, tell how the variety of word choices you identified above enhances the story.

3. _____

_____

_____

_____

_____

_____

_____

STOP

5.0

Revising
Writing

DIRECTIONS: Read about one town's centennial celebration. Use the story to answer the questions.

(1) We made a lot of preparations. (2) A cleanup committee washed all public buildings. (3) They also brushed all public buildings. (4) Members of the fire department climbed on high ladders to hang up flags and bunting. (5) Last May, our town celebrated its centennial anniversary.

(6) At last, the celebration began. (7) The high point was when Mayor Lopez asked Olga Janssen—at 105, our oldest citizen—what she remembered about the old days. (8) Mrs. Janssen recalled how her mother had used a churn to make butter, and her favorite memory was of playing dominoes with her cousins.

(9) At the end, we all drank a ginger ale toast to the town's next century. (10) We knew most of us would not be here for the next celebration, but we felt happy to be at this one. (11) A large bell was struck with a mallet by the mayor to officially close our celebration.

1. **How would you revise the first paragraph to make it read more clearly?**

   (A) Make the last sentence the first sentence.

   (B) Switch sentence 1 with sentence 2.

   (C) Delete sentence 5.

   (D) Switch sentence 1 with sentence 4.

2. **How are sentences 2 and 3 best combined?**

   (F) A cleanup committee washed all public buildings and then brushed them.

   (G) A cleanup committee washed, and they also brushed, all public buildings.

   (H) A cleanup committee washed and brushed all public buildings.

   (J) as it is

3. **How is sentence 11 best written?**

   (A) The mayor officially closed our celebration with a mallet by striking a large bell.

   (B) Striking a large bell with a mallet, our celebration officially closed by the mayor.

   (C) To officially close our celebration, the mayor struck a large bell with a mallet.

   (D) as it is

4. **Which sentence should be broken into two sentences?**

   (F) 2

   (G) 5

   (H) 8

   (J) 10

STOP

English Language Arts

6.0

Spelling Skills
Writing

DIRECTIONS: Find the word that is spelled correctly and fits best in the sentence.

Examples:

Find the word that is spelled correctly and fits best in the sentence.

A. The boat _____ toward shore.

- (A) driffed
- (B) drifded
- (C) drifted
- (D) drifteded

Answer: C

One of the underlined words is misspelled. Which answer choice is spelled incorrectly?

B.
- (F) great <u>honor</u>
- (G) <u>ackward</u> moment
- (H) bald <u>eagle</u>
- (J) dark <u>alley</u>

Answer: G

 Clue Read the directions carefully. Be sure you know if you should look for the correctly spelled word or the incorrectly spelled word.

---

1. _____ of the dog!
- (A) Beaware
- (B) Beware
- (C) Bewear
- (D) Bewaar

2. The _____ hit the moon.
- (F) asteroid
- (G) astroid
- (H) asterood
- (J) asteruod

3. He spoke with a _____ accent.
- (A) gutteral
- (B) gutterle
- (C) guttural
- (D) gutural

4. My favorite _____ is lemonade.
- (F) beaverage
- (G) beverage
- (H) bevirage
- (J) bevarage

5. The forest was _____ with color.
- (A) ablase
- (B) ableaze
- (C) ablaze
- (D) abblaze

DIRECTIONS: Read the phrases. Choose the phrase in which the underlined word is not spelled correctly.

6.
- (F) <u>horizontle</u> line
- (G) install <u>software</u>
- (H) <u>graham</u> cracker
- (J) firm <u>mattress</u>

7.
- (A) <u>invisible</u> man
- (B) <u>covert</u> operation
- (C) glove <u>compartmant</u>
- (D) <u>contagious</u> disease

8.
- (F) our <u>forfathers</u>
- (G) <u>burlap</u> sack
- (H) <u>hither</u> and yon
- (J) <u>graduating</u> senior

 GO

DIRECTIONS: Read each answer. Fill in the circle for the choice that has a spelling error. If there are no mistakes, fill in the last answer choice.

9.   Ⓐ   veer
      Ⓑ   usher
      Ⓒ   surplus
      Ⓓ   no mistakes

10.   Ⓕ   smack
      Ⓖ   stitch
      Ⓗ   toppel
      Ⓙ   no mistakes

11.   Ⓐ   patter
      Ⓑ   schedulle
      Ⓒ   mute
      Ⓓ   no mistakes

DIRECTIONS: Read each phrase. One of the underlined words is not spelled correctly for the way it is used in the phrase. Fill in the circle for the word that is not spelled correctly.

12.   Ⓕ   a <u>flare</u> for fashion
      Ⓖ   <u>bottle</u> cork
      Ⓗ   <u>hunker</u> down
      Ⓙ   <u>internal</u> medicine

13.   Ⓐ   <u>sentence</u> fragment
      Ⓑ   Earth's <u>corps</u>
      Ⓒ   cancel an <u>appointment</u>
      Ⓓ   <u>leaky</u> faucet

14.   Ⓕ   <u>subtle</u> hint
      Ⓖ   <u>sensible</u> plan
      Ⓗ   <u>except</u> an offer
      Ⓙ   food <u>staples</u>

DIRECTIONS: Find the word that is misspelled. If all the words are spelled correctly, fill in the circle for "no mistakes."

15. **The abilitie to read is a vital skill for all.**
         Ⓐ   Ⓑ   Ⓒ

     no mistakes
      Ⓓ

16. **The surly usher sneered at the boy.**
        Ⓕ   Ⓖ   Ⓗ

     no mistakes
      Ⓙ

17. **Dr. McCoy played billiards in the**
                     Ⓐ

     lounge with a formidible opponent.
        Ⓑ   Ⓒ

     no mistakes
      Ⓓ

18. **The abbot in the abbie sings alto.**
        Ⓕ   Ⓖ   Ⓗ

     no mistakes
      Ⓙ

19. **The sergeant bought the medeival memento.**
       Ⓐ   Ⓑ   Ⓒ

     no mistakes
      Ⓓ

20. **My neighbor siezed the ukulele and began to**
          Ⓕ   Ⓖ   Ⓗ

     play wildly.

     no mistakes
      Ⓙ

STOP

English Language Arts

6.0

Punctuation
Writing

DIRECTIONS: Insert the correct punctuation and capitalization in the quotations below.

> **Examples:**
>
> - When a conversation is written out, quotation marks are used around the speaker's exact words. A comma is used before the quotations when the quoted speaker's name comes first. Example: *Mark Twain said, "Always do right. This will gratify some people, and astonish the rest."*
> - When the quoted speaker's name comes last, a comma, question mark, or exclamation point is used to end the quotation. A period is used after the quoted speaker's name. Example: *"There is only one success—to be able to spend your life in your own way," said Christopher Morley.*
> - When a quotation is interrupted by the quoted speaker's name, commas are used to separate the name from the quotation. Example: *"Life is a garment we continue to alter," said David McCord, "but which never seems to fit."*
> - Colons are also used to separate clauses. Example: *The pond was right in front of her: but she couldn't stop.*
> - Semicolons are used to replace conjunctions and connect two related independent clauses. Example: *Suddenly, there was splash; all the ducks were squawking.*

1. Mark Twain said work consists of whatever a body is obliged to do. . . . Play consists of whatever a body is not obliged to do

2. April prepares her green traffic light, and the world thinks, Go said Christopher Morley

3. That's one small step for a man said Neil Armstrong and one giant leap for mankind

4. Injustice anywhere is a threat to justice everywhere said Martin Luther King, Jr.

DIRECTIONS: Correctly place commas or semicolons in the sentences below.

5. Marcy and I bolted from the car and we raced to the duck pond.

6. At first, Marcy was ahead I was behind by only a second.

7. Then, Marcy speeded up and I got out of breath.

8. Soon, Marcy passed me I didn't have a chance.

9. Marcy was really flying but she didn't look where she was going.

Examples:

- A colon is used before two or more items introduced by words such as *the following, as follows,* or *these,* or by a specific number. Examples: *For the hike, you will need the following: sturdy shoes, a backpack, and socks. There are four basic directions: north, south, east, and west.*

- A colon is not used before direct objects, predicate nouns, or objects of prepositions. Examples: *For the hike, you will need sturdy shoes, a backpack, and socks.* (direct objects) *Supplies needed for the hike are sturdy shoes, a backpack, and socks.* (predicate nouns) *She walked to the north, to the south, to the east, and to the west.* (objects of preposition)

DIRECTIONS: Rewrite the sentences below correctly.

10. **At the grocery store, we need to buy the following chicken, lettuce, and salad dressing.**

   _____

   _____

   _____

11. **Matthew likes pepperoni, onion, and green pepper: on his pizza.**

   _____

   _____

   _____

12. **There are five people: in our family Mom, Dad, Jarad, Scott, and me.**

   _____

   _____

   _____

DIRECTIONS: Correctly place missing punctuation marks at the end of or within the sentences below.

13. **The yellow daffodils are very pretty**
   - (A)   ,
   - (B)   .
   - (C)   ?
   - (D)   none

14. **The robin, our state bird, lays blue eggs.**
   - (F)   ;
   - (G)   !
   - (H)   .
   - (J)   none

15. **"Stop, she called.**
   - (A)   "
   - (B)   .
   - (C)   "
   - (D)   none

16. **We visited Michigan Ohio, and Illinois.**
   - (F)   .
   - (G)   ,
   - (H)   ;
   - (J)   none

17. **My favorite book *A Wrinkle in Time,* was already checked out.**
   - (A)   .
   - (B)   :
   - (C)   ,
   - (D)   none

STOP

English Language Arts

| 4.0–6.0 |

For pages 19–28

Mini-Test 2

Writing

DIRECTIONS: Identify the part of speech that is underlined.

1. **She lost her favorite bracelet.**
   - (A) personal pronoun
   - (B) possessive pronoun
   - (C) demonstrative pronoun
   - (D) reflexive pronoun

2. **The dog barked angrily at the salesperson.**
   - (F) adverb
   - (G) adjective
   - (H) verb
   - (J) prepositional phrase

3. **Alexis squirted ketchup on her hot dog.**
   - (A) verb
   - (B) adjective
   - (C) pronoun
   - (D) prepositional phrase

DIRECTIONS: Choose the word that is spelled correctly.

4. **Do you have any _____ foil?**
   - (F) alluminum
   - (G) aluminum
   - (H) alloominem
   - (J) aluminem

5. **My brother has to use an inhaler for his _____ .**
   - (A) asma
   - (B) asthma
   - (C) asthme
   - (D) ashma

DIRECTIONS: Choose the punctuation mark that best completes each sentence. If no punctuation is needed, choose "none."

6. **"That was great" exclaimed Stephen.**
   - (F) !
   - (G) .
   - (H) ,
   - (J) none

7. **We have band on Monday Wednesday, and Friday.**
   - (A) ;
   - (B) ,
   - (C) :
   - (D) none

DIRECTIONS: Use the paragraph below to answer the question.

(1) Lois waited for her turn to read her poem in front of the class. (2) *This is a pretty good poem,* she thought to herself. (3) *It's just that . . .* (4) Lois wondered if she had fed her dog before she left for school. (5) Then, her name was called, she stood up, and her knees began to shake. (6) When she turned around and looked at the rest of the class, however, she saw friendly faces. (7) *Maybe this won't be so bad after all,* Lois thought with relief.

8. **Which sentence should be left out of this paragraph?**
   - (F) Sentence 1
   - (G) Sentence 2
   - (H) Sentence 4
   - (J) Sentence 5

STOP

Name _____ Date _____

English Language Arts

Evaluating Information from Sources

Research

DIRECTIONS: Answer the following questions.

 Clue Not everything you read is of equal value. Some information is more accurate, up-to-date (or timely), and reliable than other information.

1. Write at least three questions you should ask yourself to determine the credibility of the information you read.

_____

_____

_____

_____

_____

_____

2. You find some old magazine articles from the 1920s speculating on the future of human flight. You also find some articles on the same topic that appeared in some aviation journals last year. Compare and evaluate the probable accuracy, timeliness, and reliability of this information.

_____

_____

_____

_____

_____

_____

3. A friend tells you that she just read an article about a scandal involving a prominent U.S. senator. She tells you that the article appeared in a supermarket tabloid. How do you respond to the story? Explain your answer.

_____

_____

_____

_____

_____

_____

4. Now, suppose your friend tells you that she got her information from *The New York Times*. Does your answer change? In what way? Why or why not?

_____

_____

_____

_____

_____

STOP

English Language Arts

| 7.0 |

Making and Questioning Hypotheses

Research

DIRECTIONS: Read the passage, and then answer the questions.

> Can you imagine a wilderness under the sea that is so humongous it has never been fully explored? The Great Barrier Reef is such a place, being the largest ridge of coral in the world. It is 1,250 miles long—that's about as far as the distance between Detroit, Michigan, and Houston, Texas. Its undersea coral gardens provide homes for more than 1,400 varieties of exotic fish. This huge maritime province stretches along the northeastern coast of Australia and ranges from 10 to more than 100 miles from the shore.

1. **Suppose you were writing a paper about the Great Barrier Reef. Based on the passage above, generate three hypotheses that you could use as the basis for research for your paper.**

   _____

   _____

   _____

   _____

   _____

   _____

2. **Based on the passage, make a guess about the types of predator fish that might exist in the Great Barrier Reef. Then, name one source you could consult to confirm your hypothesis.**

   _____

   _____

   _____

3. **Where would you be most likely to find more information about this topic?**

   (A) in an almanac

   (B) in a book describing Earth's major coral reefs

   (C) in an encyclopedia entry about the Atlantic Ocean

   (D) in an essay about agriculture in Australia

4. **Now, consult at least one source and test one of the hypotheses you made in questions 1 and 2. Briefly describe your findings.**

   _____

   _____

   _____

   _____

   _____

   _____

   _____

   _____

STOP

English Language Arts

8.0

Using Research and Technology to Support Writing

Research

DIRECTIONS: Using the Internet, find one resource of information for each topic below. For each, indicate where you found the resource (e.g., database, electronic multimedia presentation, interview, or Web site). Find each resource in a different place.

1. life in Nazi Germany

Resource: _____

Where you found the resource: _____

_____

2. the 1903 San Francisco earthquake

Resource: _____

Where you found the resource: _____

_____

3. the struggle for women's right to vote in the United States

Resource: _____

Where you found the resource: _____

_____

DIRECTIONS: Use the library or Internet to find three sources on a topic of your choice. Use different types of sources (e.g., magazines, newspapers, almanacs, encyclopedias, books, the Internet, or databases). Then, complete the information below.

4. Your topic:

_____

Description of source 1: _____

_____

Description of source 2: _____

_____

Description of source 3: _____

_____

STOP

English Language Arts

7.0–8.0

For pages 30–32

Mini-Test 3

Research

DIRECTIONS: Read the scenarios and answer the questions.

1. A respected historian claims that Thomas Jefferson had nothing whatsoever to do with the writing of the Declaration of Independence. You investigate further and learn that the historian's last book won the Pulitzer Prize for history. However, no one else has ever made this claim. How much do you trust the historian's assertion? Explain your answer.

_____

_____

_____

2. PowerCo, Inc. recently went bankrupt and the former president is accused of causing the company's failure. Last week, she wrote an editorial in *The Wall Street Journal* explaining her actions and claiming that she had nothing to do with the company's bankruptcy. This week, a team of investigative reporters at *Business Week* magazine published a detailed news story documenting her errors and bad judgment. Which do you think is a more reliable source about what really happened at PowerCo—the editorial or the news story? Why?

_____

_____

_____

DIRECTIONS: Read the passage below and then answer question 3.

As the Industrial Revolution spread throughout the United States, more and more people from other countries immigrated, or moved to, the United States. In the mid-1800s, many of the immigrants settled in the West and became farmers. But by the late 1800s, most new immigrants were settling in cities and seeking work in factories and mines.

3. Why do you suppose most new immigrants of the late 1800s and early 1900s chose to live in urban areas instead of rural areas? Name one source you could consult to confirm your hypothesis.

_____

_____

_____

4. Suppose you want to find general information about architecture and its history. Which of the following should you use?

(A) a book on world history

(B) an encyclopedia

(C) the biography of a famous architect

(D) a thesaurus

STOP

English Language Arts

| 9.0 |

Exploring Stories from Different Cultures

Cultural and Social Language Use

DIRECTIONS: The Tuskegee were a Native American nation that lived in present-day Alabama and Georgia. The passage below reflects the Tuskegee's ideas about how the earth began. Read it and then answer the questions that follow.

The Origin of Earth

Before the beginning, water was everywhere. But no people, animals, or earth were visible.

There were birds, however, who held a council to decide if it might be best to have all land or all water. "Let us have land, so we can have more food," said some of the birds. Others said, "Let's have all water, because we like it this way."

Subsequently, they appointed Eagle as their Chief who was to decide one way or the other. Eagle decided upon land and asked, "Who will go and search for land?"

Dove volunteered first and flew away. In four days, he completed his hunt and returned, reporting, "I could not find land anywhere."

Crawfish came swimming along and was asked by the council to help search for land. He disappeared under the water for four days. When he arose to the surface again, he held some dirt in his claws. He had found some land deep in the water.

Crawfish made a ball of the dirt and handed it to Chief Eagle, who then flew away with it. Four days later he returned and said to the council, "Now there is land, an island has been formed—follow me!"

The whole bird colony flew after Eagle to see the new land, though it was a very small island. Gradually, the land began to grow larger and larger as the water became lower and lower. More islands appeared and grew together, creating larger islands into one earth.

1. **What kind of story is this?**

   (A) poem

   (B) myth

   (C) fable

   (D) novel

2. **Based on this passage, you can probably conclude that the Tuskegee people _____**
.

   (F) had no religion of their own

   (G) believed they were descended from birds

   (H) had a deep respect for all creatures of nature

   (J) believed they themselves had created

Earth

3. **Many different cultures have stories about how the world was created. In the space below, tell about a creation story with which you are familiar and explain how it differs from the Tuskegee story.**

   _____

   _____

   _____

   _____

   _____

Name _____   Date _____

Writing a Critique
Cultural and Social Language Use

DIRECTIONS: Find a report you have recently written for a class. (If necessary, create a clean copy of it.) Then, exchange your report with a partner, read your partner's report, and write a critique of it. A **critique** is a critical evaluation of a piece of writing. In a critique, you discuss the strong and weak points of the writing and tell what you think about it. You might like your partner's report, dislike it, or be somewhere in the middle. But you need to explain your response.

Use the following steps to prepare your critique. When you and your partner are both finished, exchange and read the critiques. Then, meet to discuss.

Step 1. Analyze the text

Read your partner's report, taking notes on the following questions as you read:

- What is the purpose of the report (to entertain, inform, etc.)?
- What is the main point of the report?
- What arguments are given to support the main point?
- What evidence is given to support the arguments?

Step 2. Evaluate the text

Next, think about your partner's ideas. Ask yourself these questions:

- Does the report make sense?
- Is it well organized and easy to understand?
- Does the report include enough evidence to make its case?
- Does it look at both sides of the issue?
- Does it help you understand the subject?
- Are there any words or sentences that make a big impression on you? What are they? What is your reaction?
- What does the report make you think about?

Step 3. Plan and write your critique

Write your critique on a separate sheet of paper. The following outline might be useful:

   I.   Summarize your partner's purpose and main points.
   II. Analyze the accuracy, organization, and logic of the report.
   III. Agree or disagree with the ideas in the report.
   IV. Support your opinion with reasons.
   V.   Conclude by stating an overall opinion of the report.

English Language Arts

12.0

Writing to Accomplish a Purpose

Cultural and Social Language Use

DIRECTIONS: Choose the form of writing that would best suit the stated purpose.

1. **You want to tell your aunt about your science fair project.**
   - (A) a personal letter
   - (B) a report
   - (C) a business letter
   - (D) a letter to the editor

2. **You want to encourage the citizens in your community to vote for the school bond levy.**
   - (F) a personal letter
   - (G) a letter to the editor
   - (H) a report
   - (J) a review

3. **You want to share your feelings about a beautiful sunset.**
   - (A) a poem
   - (B) a letter to the editor
   - (C) a review
   - (D) a report

4. **You want to tell others about the special effects, script, and acting in a new science fiction movie you just watched.**
   - (F) a personal letter
   - (G) a review
   - (H) a poem
   - (J) a letter to the editor

5. **You want to apply for a position as summer camp counselor.**
   - (A) a poem
   - (B) a letter to the editor
   - (C) a business letter
   - (D) a personal letter

6. **You want to inform your classmates about the history of skateboarding.**
   - (F) a business letter
   - (G) a review
   - (H) a personal letter
   - (J) a report

DIRECTIONS: Write a paragraph to persuade your teacher to take your class on an outing to a local amusement park.

7. _____

_____

_____

_____

_____

_____

_____

_____

_____

_____

_____

_____

_____

_____

_____

_____

_____

STOP

English Language Arts

9.0–12.0

For pages 34–36

Mini-Test 4

Cultural and Social Language Use

DIRECTIONS: Read the following story that was told by the ancient Greeks. Then, answer the questions.

Daedalus

A builder named Daedalus lived with his son Icarus on the island of Crete. Daedalus designed the labyrinth, a maze of complicated passages that is very difficult to escape. Minos, the king of Crete, used the labyrinth to hide a monster called Minotaur, who was half-man and half-bull.

Daedalus did something to anger Minos, and the king made Daedalus and Icarus prisoners in the labyrinth. One day, Daedalus got an idea as he was watching birds fly. He asked Icarus to gather up all the bird feathers he could find. Then, using the feathers and some wax, Daedalus created two large pairs of wings. Soon, he and Icarus were on their way over the walls of the labyrinth.

1. **What kind of story is this?**

    (A) poem

    (B) myth

    (C) fable

    (D) novel

2. **From this story, you can conclude that the ancient Greeks _____ .**

    (F) believed that people could fly

    (G) only told stories about real people

    (H) liked to hide in labyrinths

    (J) had a rich story-telling tradition

DIRECTIONS: Choose the form of writing that would best suit the author's stated purpose.

3. **The author wants to tell her grandmother about her experiences at summer camp.**

    (A) a business letter

    (B) a personal letter

    (C) a letter to the editor

    (D) a poem

4. **The author wants to describe the beauty of a winter landscape.**

    (F) a letter to the editor

    (G) a review

    (H) a poem

    (J) a report

5. **The author wants to convince more people in her town to attend school-board meetings.**

    (A) a review

    (B) a report

    (C) a personal letter

    (D) a letter to the editor

6. **Write a paragraph to convince your friends that it is important to volunteer.**

    _____

    _____

    _____

    _____

    _____

    _____

    _____

STOP

How Am I Doing?

Mini-Test 1

Page 18

Number Correct

5 answers correct	**Great Job!** Move on to the section test on page 40.
4 answers correct	**You're almost there!** But you still need a little practice. Review practice pages 9–17 before moving on to the section test on page 40.
0–3 answers correct	**Oops!** Time to review what you have learned and try again. Review the practice section on pages 9–17. Then, retake the test on page 18. Now, move on to the section test on page 40.

Mini-Test 2

Page 29

Number Correct

7–8 answers correct	**Awesome!** Move on to the section test on page 40.
5–6 answers correct	**You're almost there!** But you still need a little practice. Review practice pages 19–28 before moving on to the section test on page 40.
0–4 answers correct	**Oops!** Time to review what you have learned and try again. Review the practice section on pages 19–28. Then, retake the test on page 29. Now, move on to the section test on page 40.

Mini-Test 3

Page 33

Number Correct

4 answers correct	**Great Job!** Move on to the section test on page 40.
3 answers correct	**You're almost there!** But you still need a little practice. Review practice pages 30–32 before moving on to the section test on page 40.
0–2 answers correct	**Oops!** Time to review what you have learned and try again. Review the practice section on pages 30–32. Then, retake the test on page 33. Now, move on to the section test on page 40.

How Am I Doing?

Mini-Test 4	**6** answers correct	**Terrific!** Move on to the section test on page 40.
Page 37 **Number Correct**	**5** answers correct	**You're almost there!** But you still need a little practice. Review practice pages 34–36 before moving on to the section test on page 40.
	0–4 answers correct	**Oops!** Time to review what you have learned and try again. Review the practice section on pages 34–36. Then, retake the test on page 37. Now, move on to the section test on page 40.

Name _____   Date _____

Final English Language Arts Test
for pages 9–36

DIRECTIONS: Read the following passage. Then, answer the questions.

One afternoon in March, I found two silver dollars shining in a half-melted snow bank. I instantly thought of buried treasure. So I dug through the snow searching for more. All I ended up with were two really cold hands. I slipped the two coins in my pocket and went home colder but richer.

The next morning, Megan and her little sister were searching the snow banks. *Finders keepers* was my first thought. I didn't need to add the *losers weepers* part since Moira was already crying for real. "I dropped them right here," she said between tears. Her hands were red from digging in the snow. "Maybe they got shoved down the street by the snow plow. Let's try over there," Megan said optimistically.

They'll never know was my second thought, as I walked past them toward Tyler's house.

"Phil, have you seen two silver dollars?" Megan called. Moira looked up from the snow bank with hope bright in her eyes.

"Coins?" *Look innocent* was my third thought.

"Yes, Moira dropped two silver dollars somewhere around here yesterday."

"Yeah," said Moira, "they're big and heavy." She brushed her icy red hands off on her jacket and wiped the tears from her eyes. Her eyes were as red as her hands.

I hesitated, but only for a moment. Then, I said, "As a matter of fact, I dug two coins out of that snow bank yesterday. I wondered who might have lost them." Moira ran to me and gave me a bear hug. "Oh, thank you, thank you!" she cried. I couldn't help but smile.

1. What is the setting of this story?

(A) outside on a March day

(B) outside on a warm, sunny day

(C) inside on a rainy spring day

(D) the view outside a window

2. What is the theme of this story?

(F) It is okay to lie if you think you will get away with it.

(G) It is always better to be honest than rich.

(H) "Finders keepers, losers weepers" is not a good saying to live by.

(J) both G and H

3. What images from the story convey that Moira has been searching for the coins for a long time?

(A) Moira is crying.

(B) Moira says the coins are big and heavy.

(C) Megan is optimistic.

(D) Moira's hands are red and cold from digging.

4. Overall, what type of person is Phil?

(F) ambitious and unfair

(G) honest and caring

(H) greedy and cruel

(J) dishonest and angry

DIRECTIONS: Read the following passage, and then answer the questions.

Maternal Fish Father

In the warm and temperate waters of the world live two unusual fish: the sea horse and its relative, the pipefish.

The sea horse, so-called because its head resembles a horse, is a small fish about two to eight inches long. It swims by moving the dorsal fin on its back. It is the only fish with a prehensile tail that it uses, like a monkey, to coil around and cling to seaweed.

The pipefish is named for its long snout, which looks like a thin pipe. When its body is straight, the pipefish resembles a slender snake. Its body forms an S shape and is propelled by its rear fins.

GO ▷

But it is not appearance that makes the sea horse and pipefish unique. It is their paternal roles. With both fish, the female's responsibility ends when she lays and deposits her eggs. From that point on, the male takes over and, in a manner of speaking, gives birth to the babies.

Both the male sea horse and pipefish have pouch-like organs on their undersides in which the female deposits her eggs. Here the young fish stay and are nourished for either a few days or for several weeks, depending on the species. When the baby sea horses are ready to be born, the father sea horse attaches itself to a plant and actually goes through the pangs of childbirth. As the sea horse bends back and forth, the wall of its brood pouch contracts. With each spasm, a baby fish is introduced into the world of the sea. The birth of the baby pipefish is less dramatic. The father's pouch simply opens, and the offspring swim off on their own.

5. What is the main idea of this passage?

Ⓐ   The pipefish and the sea horse fathers are unusual because of the way their offspring are born.

Ⓑ   Sea horses resemble horses but have tails like monkeys.

Ⓒ   Female pipefish and sea horses are lazy.

Ⓓ   Sea horses make good pets.

6. To what genre does this passage belong?

Ⓕ   fiction

Ⓖ   nonfiction

Ⓗ   myth

Ⓙ   biography

7. What is the author's purpose?

Ⓐ   to compare and contrast two fish

Ⓑ   to entertain

Ⓒ   to persuade

Ⓓ   to confuse

DIRECTIONS: Choose the form of writing that would best suit the author's stated purpose.

8. The author wants to describe her vacation in Italy.

Ⓕ   a persuasive essay

Ⓖ   a report

Ⓗ   a business letter

Ⓙ   a personal letter

9. The author wants to convince her classmates to recycle.

Ⓐ   a review

Ⓑ   a report

Ⓒ   a personal letter

Ⓓ   a persuasive essay

DIRECTIONS: Identify the part of speech that is underlined.

10. The cat quickly scurried up the tree.

Ⓕ   adverb

Ⓖ   adjective

Ⓗ   preposition

Ⓙ   verb

11. Dana's favorite foods are apple pie and ice cream.

Ⓐ   verb

Ⓑ   adjective

Ⓒ   pronoun

Ⓓ   adverb

12. Kayla quickly finished her homework.

Ⓕ   verb

Ⓖ   noun

Ⓗ   pronoun

Ⓙ   adverb

GO

DIRECTIONS: Choose the answer that shows correct punctuation. If no punctuation is needed, choose "correct as is."

13. My favorite place to visit is New York City which is known as the Big Apple.

    (A) New York City; which

    (B) New York City, which

    (C) New York City: which

    (D) correct as is

14. I grew up in Cincinnati, Ohio my dad grew up in Chicago.

    (F) Ohio, my

    (G) Ohio: my

    (H) Ohio; my

    (J) correct as is

DIRECTIONS: Choose the best answer.

15. Which of the following is probably the most reliable source of information about the effect of nutrition on the human body?

    (A) *Sports Illustrated*

    (B) a supermarket tabloid

    (C) a movie star's statement on a TV talk show

    (D) *The New England Journal of Medicine*

16. Which of the following is the most likely place to find the results of last week's school-board elections in your county?

    (F) a book about the history of your state

    (G) your local newspaper

    (H) an encyclopedia

    (J) *Time* magazine

DIRECTIONS: Choose the phrase in which the underlined word is not spelled correctly.

17.   (A) our <u>residance</u>

    (B) <u>adhesive</u> tape

    (C) compose a <u>sonnet</u>

    (D) nouns and <u>adjectives</u>

18.   (F) sit on the <u>balcony</u>

    (G) the <u>abominible</u> snowman

    (H) <u>alkaline</u> battery

    (J) the dog <u>yelped</u>

DIRECTIONS: Read the passage and answer the questions.

(1) Kerry was always wary of his brother—listening for footsteps or watching for flying objects such as books, toys, or sticks. (2) Kerry had to keep his eyes open. (3) He also had to keep his ears open at all times. (4) Although Kerry and Jimmy were only a year apart, the boys were as different as Laurel and Hardy or Fred and Barney. (5) Jimmy, the older brother, was in seventh grade and was already six-feet tall and weighed 180 pounds. (6) But his mom loved him and thought he was a good boy. (7) Jimmy was especially frightening today because he had a temper. (8) Today was the day of the annual race between the sixth and seventh graders. (9) The sixth graders were sure to win. (10) What Kerry lacked in size, he made up for in speed. (11) He was the fastest runner in the school. (12) And that was the problem—Jimmy would be furious.

19. How are sentences 2 and 3 best combined?

    (A) Kerry had to keep his eyes open, and he had to keep his ears open at all times.

    (B) At all times, Kerry had to keep open his eyes and his ears also.

    (C) Kerry at all times had to keep his eyes open and his ears also.

    (D) Kerry had to keep his eyes and ears open at all times.

20. Which sentence does not belong in this story?

    (F) sentence 4

    (G) sentence 6

    (H) sentence 7

    (J) sentence 12

Final English Language Arts Test

Answer Sheet

1 (A) (B) (C) (D)
2 (F) (G) (H) (J)
3 (A) (B) (C) (D)
4 (F) (G) (H) (J)
5 (A) (B) (C) (D)
6 (F) (G) (H) (J)
7 (A) (B) (C) (D)
8 (F) (G) (H) (J)
9 (A) (B) (C) (D)
10 (F) (G) (H) (J)

11 (A) (B) (C) (D)
12 (F) (G) (H) (J)
13 (A) (B) (C) (D)
14 (F) (G) (H) (J)
15 (A) (B) (C) (D)
16 (F) (G) (H) (J)
17 (A) (B) (C) (D)
18 (F) (G) (H) (J)
19 (A) (B) (C) (D)
20 (F) (G) (H) (J)

Mathematics Standards

Standard 1—Number and Operations *(See pages 45–49.)*
  A. Understand numbers, ways of representing numbers, relationships among numbers, and number systems.
  B. Understand meanings of operations and how they relate to one another.
  C. Compute fluently and make reasonable estimates.

Standard 2—Algebra *(See pages 50–54.)*
  A. Understand patterns, relations, and functions.
  B. Represent and analyze mathematical situations and structures using algebraic symbols.
  C. Use mathematical models to represent and understand quantitative relationships.
  D. Analyze change in various contexts.

Standard 3—Geometry *(See pages 56–60.)*
  A. Analyze characteristics and properties of two- and three-dimensional shapes and develop mathematical arguments about geometric relationships.
  B. Specify locations and describe spatial relationships using coordinate geometry and other representational systems.
  C. Apply transformations and use symmetry to analyze mathematical situations.
  D. Use visualization, spatial reasoning, and geometric modeling to solve problems.

Standard 4—Measurement *(See pages 61–64.)*
  A. Understand measurable attributes of objects and the units, systems, and processes of measurement.
  B. Apply appropriate techniques, tools, and formulas to determine measurement.

Standard 5—Data Analysis and Probability *(See pages 66–69.)*
  A. Formulate questions that can be addressed with data and collect, organize, and display relevant data to answer them.
  B. Select and use appropriate statistical methods to analyze data.
  C. Develop and evaluate inferences and predictions that are based on data.
  D. Understand and apply basic concepts of probability.

Standard 6—Process *(See pages 70–73.)*
  A. Problem Solving
  B. Reasoning and Proof
  C. Communication
  D. Connections
  E. Representation

Mathematics

| 1.A |

Understanding Functions
Number and Operations

DIRECTIONS: Complete the table for each function rule given below.

1. Rule: $m = n + 3$

IN(n)	12	14	16	18	20	22
OUT(m)	15	17	19			

2. Rule: $m = 3n$

IN(n)	0	1	2	3	4	5
OUT(m)						

3. Rule: $m = 3n - 3$

IN(n)	2	4	6	8	10	12
OUT(m)						

DIRECTIONS: Find the function rule for each table below.

4.

IN(x)	6	7	9	11	14	16
OUT(y)	10	11	13	15	18	20

Rule: $y =$ _____

5.

IN(x)	1	3	6	8	10	13
OUT(y)	4	12	24	32	40	52

Rule: $y =$ _____

6.

IN(x)	10	13	16	19	22	25
OUT(y)	8	11	14	17	20	23

Rule: $y =$ _____

STOP

Mathematics

| 1.A |

Analyzing Algorithms
Number and Operations

DIRECTIONS: Use the algorithms described below in each example box to choose the best answers.

Example:

One algorithm for dividing fractions is: (1) Flip the second fraction to get its reciprocal. Then, multiply the numerators and the denominators to find the answer. *Example:* To find $\frac{10}{12} \div \frac{2}{4}$, flip $\frac{2}{4}$ to get $\frac{4}{2}$. Then, multiply 10×4 and 12×2, which gives you $\frac{40}{24}$.

1. $\frac{9}{10} \div \frac{1}{5} =$

(A) $\frac{4}{2}$ (C) $\frac{8}{5}$

(B) $\frac{9}{2}$ (D) $\frac{2}{9}$

2. $\frac{5}{14} \div \frac{1}{2} =$

(F) $\frac{4}{12}$ (H) $\frac{5}{7}$

(G) $\frac{7}{5}$ (J) $\frac{1}{3}$

Example:

One algorithm for converting mixed numbers to fractions is: (1) multiply the whole number and the denominator, (2) add the numerator to the sum to find the new numerator, and (3) place the new numerator over the original denominator. *Example:* To convert $7\frac{1}{3}$ to a fraction, multiply $7 \times 3 = 21$; add the sum to the numerator: $21 + 1 = 22$; and place the new numerator over the original denominator: $\frac{22}{3}$.

3. $8\frac{3}{4} =$

(A) $\frac{24}{3}$ (C) $\frac{32}{4}$

(B) $\frac{24}{4}$ (D) $\frac{35}{4}$

4. $7\frac{5}{6} =$

(F) $\frac{35}{6}$ (H) $\frac{42}{6}$

(G) $\frac{35}{5}$ (J) $\frac{47}{6}$

Example:

One algorithm for multiplying two numbers is: (1) break down one of the numbers into a simpler equation, (2) multiply the first number by the new second number, and (3) multiply the result by the new third number. *Example:* To multiply 25×36, break down one of the numbers into a simpler equation: $25 \times 4 \times 9$; multiply the first number by the new second number: $25 \times 4 = 100$; and multiply that result by the new third number: $100 \times 9 = 900$.

5. $12 \times 15 =$

(A) 160   (C) 200

(B) 180   (D) 220

6. **20×25 is the same as**

_____ .

(F) $20 \times 5 \times 5$

(G) $20 \times 20 \times 5$

(H) $10 \times 10 \times 25$

(J) $20 \times 4 \times 5$

STOP

Name _____ Date _____

Mathematics

Using Properties of Numbers
Number and Operations

DIRECTIONS: Choose the best answer.

The **commutative property** says you can switch the order of the numbers and still get the same answer. The **associative property** says you can change the grouping of the numbers and still get the same answer. The **distributive property** is used when there is a combination of multiplication over addition or subtraction.

1. **According to the distributive property, which of the following is the same as $5(x + 3)$?**

   (A) $5x + 3$

   (B) $5x + 5 \times 3$

   (C) $5 + 3x$

   (D) $5x - 3$

2. **According to the distributive property, which of the following is the same as $2(7x + 4) - 5$?**

   (F) $2(7) + (x + 4) - 5$

   (G) $2(7x) + 2(-1)$

   (H) $2(7x) + 2(4) - 5$

   (J) $2(7x) + 2(4) - (2 \times 5)$

3. **The commutative property applies to which types of operations?**

   (A) addition

   (B) multiplication

   (C) division

   (D) both A and B

4. **Identify the property that makes the number sentence $(46 + 78) + 23 = 46 + (78 + 23)$ true.**

   (F) distributive

   (G) commutative

   (H) associative

   (J) both F and G

The **identity property of addition** states that the sum of any number and zero is the original number. The **identity property of multiplication** states that the product of any number and one is that number. **Inverse operations** are operations that undo each other.

DIRECTIONS: Indicate if the equation illustrates the identity property of addition or multiplication by writing a **Y** in the appropriate space. If it does not, write an **N** in the appropriate space.

_____ 5. $5 + 0 = 5$

_____ 6. $5 + 7 = 7 + 5$

_____ 7. $18 \times 1 = 18$

_____ 8. $0 + a = a$

_____ 9. $5(4 + 5) = (5 \times 4) + (5 \times 5)$

DIRECTIONS: Write the inverse of each of the following.

10. $+ 7$ _____

11. $- 15$ _____

12. $\div 3$ _____

13. $\times 7$ _____

14. $+ 6$ _____

15. $\times 9$ _____

STOP

Mathematics
1.B

Multiplying and Dividing Fractions and Mixed Numbers
Number and Operations

DIRECTIONS: Multiply the following fractions and mixed numbers. Reduce the mixed numbers to their lowest terms.

1. $\dfrac{4}{7} \times \dfrac{2}{3} =$

2. $\dfrac{5}{8} \times \dfrac{1}{6} =$

3. $\dfrac{1}{2} \times \dfrac{3}{5} =$

4. $2\dfrac{2}{3} \times 3\dfrac{1}{4} =$

5. $3\dfrac{7}{9} \times 1\dfrac{7}{8} =$

6. $4\dfrac{2}{8} \times 5\dfrac{3}{5} =$

7. $4\dfrac{1}{3} \times 7\dfrac{1}{2} =$

8. $5\dfrac{3}{8} \times 4\dfrac{3}{4} =$

9. $\dfrac{6}{7} \times 5\dfrac{2}{8} =$

DIRECTIONS: Divide the following fractions and mixed numbers. Reduce the answers to their lowest terms.

10. $\dfrac{4}{5} \div \dfrac{2}{5} =$

11. $1\dfrac{1}{2} \div 18 =$

12. $0 \div \dfrac{2}{3} =$

13. $1 \div 7\dfrac{1}{2} =$

14. $\dfrac{9}{10} \div \dfrac{1}{5} =$

15. $4\dfrac{2}{5} \div \dfrac{1}{4} =$

16. $4\dfrac{1}{2} \div 18 =$

17. $\dfrac{5}{14} \div \dfrac{1}{2} =$

18. $4\dfrac{1}{3} \div \dfrac{26}{27} =$

STOP

Name _____   Date _____

Mathematics

Using Ratios to Solve Problems

Number and Operations

DIRECTIONS: Analyze the following problems and determine whether they can be solved using ratios. If so, write **Y** in the blank space; if not, write **N**.

A **ratio** is a comparison of one quantity to another.

_____ 1. "Now batting for Toledo, Mickey Calavito," the game announcer yells into his microphone. In the last game, Mickey got 1 hit in 4 tries. If he continues to hit at this rate, determine how many hits Mickey can expect to get if he bats 600 times during the season.

_____ 2. The 154 sixth graders at Ellison Middle School sold an average of 38 tickets each for the school's annual raffle, which raises money to buy additional library books. The cost of each raffle ticket was $4. How much money was raised for the library?

_____ 3. Aleesha saved $0.45 a week out of her allowance for several weeks so that she could buy a bottle of nail polish for $2.70. How many weeks did she need to save $0.45?

_____ 4. Richard sits at a table in the cafeteria with his 7 friends. Usually, his friends are all hungry enough to order the full lunch menu, but today, only two of his friends order the full lunch menu. There are 332 students in the cafeteria. If Richard's table is representative of the entire cafeteria, how many students in the cafeteria ordered the full lunch menu?

_____ 5. Forty percent of the class finished their assignment before lunch. There are 25 students in the class. How many students finished before lunch?

_____ 6. Fred is drawing a scale model of a room that is 12 feet by 14 feet. If he makes one side of the room 3 inches, how long should the other side be?

_____ 7. The temperature in Rockville at 7:00 A.M. was 7°C. By 12:00 noon, the temperature increased to 13°C, but it fell by 3°C by 6:00 P.M. How much did the temperature increase between 7:00 A.M. and noon?

_____ 8. Kerri worked out for $1\frac{1}{2}$ hours, Kelly worked out for 2 hours, and Briana worked out for 45 minutes. What was the total workout time for all three women?

STOP

2.A

Comparing Equations
Algebra

DIRECTIONS: On the blanks next to each number sentence, write **T** if the sentence is true and **F** if the sentence is false.

_____ 1. $8 + 4 = 6 \times 2$

_____ 2. $\frac{27}{9} = 0 \times 3$

_____ 3. $21 \times 3 = 60 + 3$

_____ 4. $12 \times 3 = 9 \times 4$

_____ 5. $8 + 7 = 14 \times 2$

_____ 6. $18 \times 2 = 9 \times 2 + 2$

_____ 7. $56 - y = (7 \times 8) - y$

_____ 8. $3 \times a = 3 - 1 \times a$

_____ 9. $16 + x = 10 + 6 + x$

_____ 10. $m + m = 2(m)$

_____ 11. $n + 6(3 - 1) = 15 + n$

_____ 12. $(y \times 8) + 5 = 23 - y$

_____ 13. $n^2 + 5 = 18 - n$

_____ 14. $25 - p = 15 + p$

_____ 15. $3y + 1 = 29 - y$

DIRECTIONS: For each number sentence below, write $<$, $>$, or $=$ in the box to make the sentence true.

16. $30 + 40 \ \square \ 50 + 21$

17. $\frac{1}{2} \times 50 \ \square \ 20 + 30$

18. $42 \times 2 \ \square \ 20 \times 4$

19. $3(4 + 2) \ \square \ 9 \times 2$

20. $71 - 45 \ \square \ 3 \times 10$

21. $49 \div 7 \ \square \ \frac{40}{10}$

22. $54 \times 2 \ \square \ 31 \times 3$

23. $75 \div 25 \ \square \ 60 \div 30$

24. $\frac{2}{3} \times \frac{2}{4} \ \square \ \frac{30}{90}$

25. $4(12 - 5) \ \square \ 5(10 - 5)$

26. $62 - 50 \ \square \ 3(8 - 4)$

27. $23 \times 3 \ \square \ 15 \times 4$

28. $48 \div 6 \ \square \ 2 \times 8$

29. $4^2 + 5 \ \square \ 42 \div 2$

30. $5(12 + 7) \ \square \ 12 \times 8$

31. $11 \times 12 \ \square \ 4^3 \times 2$

STOP

Mathematics

2.B

Using Variables and Equal Symbols

Algebra

DIRECTIONS: Evaluate the following expressions if $w = \frac{1}{3}$, $y = 4$, and $z = -2$.

> **Example:**
>
> Let $w = -2$, $y = 3$, and $z = \frac{1}{2}$
>
> Then, $w(2z - 4y) = -2(2 \times \frac{1}{2} - 4 \times 3)$
>
> $\qquad\qquad = -2(1 - 12)$
>
> $\qquad\qquad = -2 \times -11$
>
> $\qquad\qquad = 22$

1. $3w = $ _____

2. $y + z = $ _____

3. $y - z = $ _____

4. $w(8 + y) = $ _____

5. $6zw = $ _____

6. $3(y + z) - 6w = $ _____

DIRECTIONS: Evaluate the following expressions if $a = -3$, $b = 8$, and $c = \frac{1}{2}$.

7. $4a + 3b = $ _____

8. $(2a - b)c = $ _____

9. $2(a + b) - 10c = $ _____

10. $b[(12c - 3a)2 - 10] = $ _____

11. $(a - b)2c + b + 2a = $ _____

12. $(a + 2c)(b - 5) = $ _____

STOP

Mathematics

2.B

Equivalent Open Sentences
Algebra

DIRECTIONS: Choose the best answer.

Clue   A **solution set** is the answer that makes an open sentence true.

1. Which of the following open sentences has the same solution set as $21 - n = 10$?
   - (A) $n = 5 \times 2 - 1$
   - (B) $12 + n = 26$
   - (C) $30 - n = 21$
   - (D) $n = 10 + 1$

2. Which of the following open sentences have the same solution set?
   - (F) $6 + n = 18; 20 - n = 18$
   - (G) $12 \div n = 27; n \div 3 = 6$
   - (H) $18 \div n = 3; 4n = 24$
   - (J) $25 - n = 16; n + 8 = 16$

3. Which of the following open sentences have the same solution set?
   - (A) $6 + x = x + 5 + 1$
   - (B) $5(2 + x) = 5(2) - 5(x)$
   - (C) $6 + 2x = 6 + 2 + x$
   - (D) $9 - x = 9(x)$

4. Which of the following open sentences have the same solution set?
   - (F) $4 + y = 10 - y$
   - (G) $4(y + 2) = 4(y) + 8$
   - (H) $5 \times y = 2 \times 3 + y$
   - (J) $0 + y = 0y$

5. Which of the following open sentences has the same solution set as $4 + z = 16$?
   - (A) $z(2 + 2) = 36$
   - (B) $z(2) + 2 = 12$
   - (C) $z \times 2 - 5 = 19$
   - (D) $4 - 2 + z = 10$

6. Which of the following open sentences has the same solution set as $15 \times r = 75$?
   - (F) $4r = 20$
   - (G) $r + 15 = 18$
   - (H) $21 - r = 15$
   - (J) $36 \div r = 9$

7. Which of the following open sentences has the same solution set as $n + 12 = 35$?
   - (A) $46 \div n = 2$
   - (B) $n - 10 = 10$
   - (C) $n \times 3 = 45$
   - (D) $105 \div n = 5$

STOP

Mathematics

2.C

Graphing Simple Inequalities
Algebra

DIRECTIONS: For each question, shade the correct points on the number line to solve the inequality.

Clue To solve an inequality is to find all values of the variable that make the inequality true.

1. On this number line, shade all the points on the line where $x + 2 < 7$.

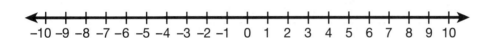

2. On this number line, shade all the points on the line where $x > 5$.

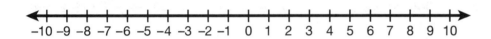

3. On this number line, shade all the points on the line where $x \geq 5$.

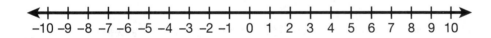

4. On this number line, shade all the points on the line where $x + 2 < -3$.

5. On this number line, shade all the points on the line where $x + 6 \geq -4$.

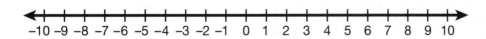

STOP

Name _____ Date _____

2.D

Using Graphs for Linear Equations

Algebra

DIRECTIONS: Solve each problem.

Clue The **Cartesian plane** is a plane with a coordinate system that associates each point on the plane with a pair of numbers. The first number in the pair identifies the point on the *x*-axis and the second number identifies the point on the *y*-axis.

1. **For the linear equation *y* = 3*x* + 2, find the corresponding *y* values when *x* = −3, −2, −1, 0, 1, 2, and 3. Show the results as a table of values.**

x							
y							

2. **For the linear equation *y* = 2*x*, find the corresponding *y* values when *x* = −3, −2, −1, 0, 1, 2, and 3. Show the results as a table of values.**

x							
y							

3. **Plot the points on the Cartesian plane for the equation given in question 1.**

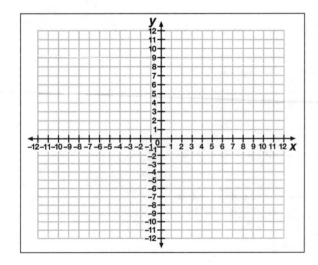

4. **Plot the points on the Cartesian plane for the equation given in question 2.**

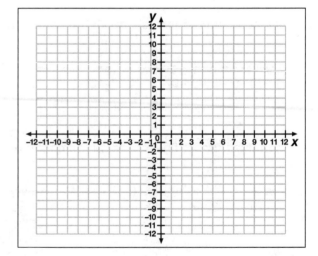

STOP

Name _____   Date _____

Mini-Test 1

Number and Operations; Algebra

DIRECTIONS: Choose the best answer.

1. **Identify the property that makes the following number sentence true.**

   $(10 + 5) + 6 = 10 + (5 + 6)$

   - (A) commutative
   - (B) distributive
   - (C) associative
   - (D) both A and C

2. **Which of the following is the inverse of + 16?**

   - (F) $- 16$
   - (G) $\times 16$
   - (H) $\div 16$
   - (J) 4^2

3. **Which of the following open sentences has the same solution set as $17 + x = 30$?**

   - (A) $x - 10 = 5$
   - (B) $5x = 60$
   - (C) $x + 33 = 45$
   - (D) $78 \div x = 6$

4. **Which of the following number sentences is true?**

   - (F) $50 - 26 < 4 \times 7$
   - (G) $2(3 + 5) = 4 \times 5$
   - (H) $3(8 - 2) > 42 - 21$
   - (J) $\frac{2}{3} \times 15 < \frac{1}{2} \times 16$

5. $10 \div 3\frac{1}{3} =$

   - (A) $3\frac{1}{2}$
   - (B) 3
   - (C) $2\frac{2}{3}$
   - (D) $3\frac{1}{5}$

DIRECTIONS: Choose the best answer.

6. **Consider the table of values shown. The relationship of x to y is represented by which equation?**

x	0	1	2	3	4
y	2	5	8	11	14

   - (F) $y = 4x$
   - (G) $y = x + 2$
   - (H) $y = 3x + 2$
   - (J) $y = 4x - 1$

7. **The line is the graph for—**

   - (A) $x = y$
   - (B) $x = y + 4$
   - (C) $x = 8y$
   - (D) $x = y + 2$

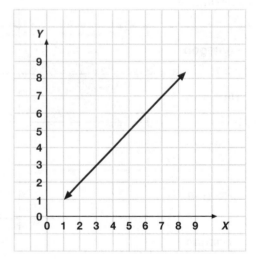

8. **Evaluate $3x - y$ if $x = 4$ and $y = 1$.**

   - (F) 11
   - (G) 12
   - (H) 6
   - (J) 9

STOP

Mathematics

3.A

Finding Geometric Relationships
Geometry

DIRECTIONS: Complete the table below.

Examples:

- To find the number of diagonals in a polygon, use the following formula: $n(n - 3) \div 2$.
- To find the number of interior triangles in a polygon, use the following formula: $n - 2$.
- To find the sum of the angles in a polygon, use the following formula: $t \times 180$.

n = number of polygon sides
t = number of interior triangles

 Clue A **diagonal** is a line segment that connects nonadjacent vertices in a polygon.

Name	Sides	Diagonals	Interior Triangles	Sum of Angles
Quadrilateral				
Pentagon				
Hexagon				
Heptagon				
Octagon				
Nonagon				
Decagon				
Dodecagon				

Classifying Triangles
Geometry

DIRECTIONS: Look at each triangle. Write the type of triangle (*right, acute,* or *obtuse*) on the line. Then, write the measurement of the missing angle. The first one is done for you.

Clue The angle measures in a triangle always add up to 180°. A **right** triangle has one 90° angle. An **obtuse** triangle has one angle that is greater than 90°. An **acute** triangle has all three angles less than 90°.

1.

30°

right 60°

2.

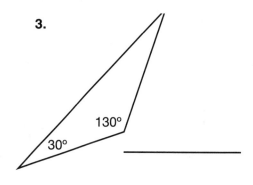

45°

25°

_____

3.

130°

30°

_____

4.

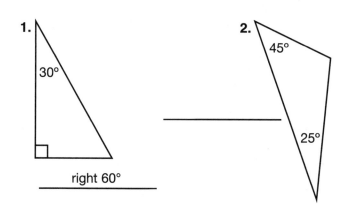

64°

80°

_____

5.

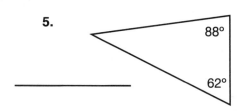

88°

62°

_____

6.

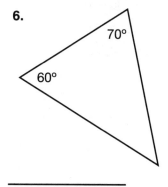

70°

60°

_____

7.

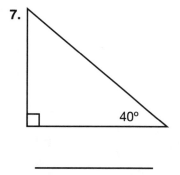

40°

_____

8.

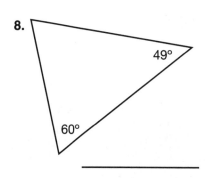

49°

60°

_____

STOP

Name _____   Date _____

Using Ordered Pairs to Construct Figures

Geometry

DIRECTIONS: Plot the points to create four figures on the graph. Connect points with line segments in the order given (go down the columns).

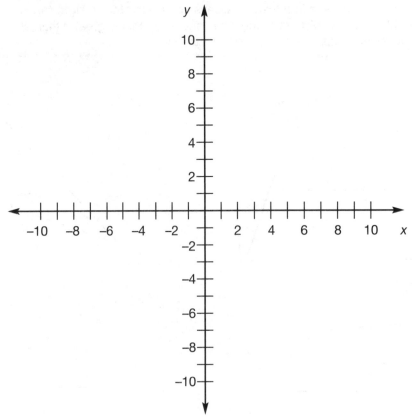

Figure 1	Figure 2	Figure 3	Figure 4
(–7, 1)	(7, 1)	(–7, –2)	(5, –5)
(–5, 1)	(7, 3)	(–7, –5)	(5, –4)
(–5, 3)	(5, 3)	(–6, –5)	(4, –4)
(–3, 3)	(5, 5)	(–6, –4)	(4, –3)
(–3, 1)	(7, 5)	(–5, –4)	(5, –3)
(–1, 1)	(7, 7)	(–5, –5)	(5, –2)
(–1, 7)	(1, 7)	(–4, –5)	(2, –2)
(–3, 7)	(1, 5)	(–4, –2)	(2, –3)
(–3, 5)	(3, 5)	(–5, –2)	(3, –3)
(–5, 5)	(3, 3)	(–5, –3)	(3, –4)
(–5, 7)	(1, 3)	(–6, –3)	(2, –4)
(–7, 7)	(1, 1)	(–6, –2)	(2, –5)
(–7, 1)	(7, 1)	(–7, –2)	(5, –5)

STOP

Name _____ Date _____

Transformations
Geometry

DIRECTIONS: Compare the following images to their transformation images. What type of transformation was performed? Be as specific as possible.

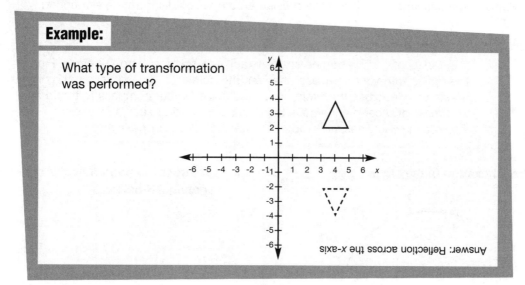

Example:

What type of transformation was performed?

Answer: Reflection across the x-axis

1. _____

2. _____

3. _____

4. _____

5. _____

6. _____

STOP

Mathematics

3.D

Performing
Simple Constructions
Geometry

DIRECTIONS: Perform the constructions as indicated using a compass, ruler, or mira, as needed.

 **Clue** The radius of a circle can be struck exactly six times around the circle. Find the radius with your compass, then set the point of the compass on the circle. Make a mark across the circle, move the point of your compass to that mark, and make another mark across the circle. Connecting each successive intersection with lines will produce a six-sided figure or hexagon.

1. **Inscribe a hexagon in the circle below.**

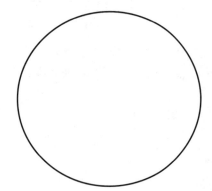

2. **Construct an angle bisector of the angle below.**

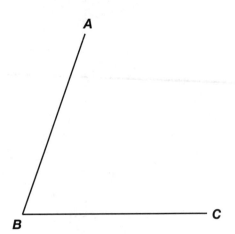

3. **Construct the perpendicular bisector of segment *AB* below.**

A •————————————————————• B

4. **Construct a circle that includes the vertices of triangle *STU* below.**

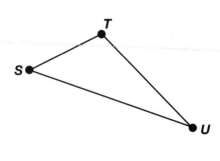

Mathematics

| 4.A |

Capacity
Measurements–Metric
Measurement

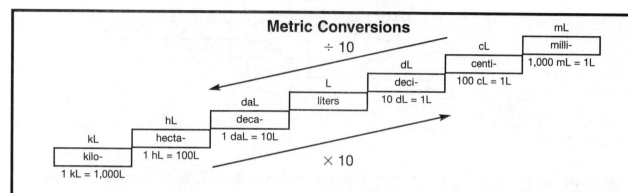

Metric Conversions

÷ 10

× 10

Multiply when moving up on the chart—from kiloliters to liters or from liters to centiliters. Divide when moving down on the chart—from milliliters to deciliters or from meters to hectaliters.

Smaller Units to Larger Units	**Larger Units to Smaller Units**
5,700 mL = _____ L	_____ cL = 7.38 hL
To get from milliliters to liters, you must move down three stairs. So, divide by 10^3 (or 1,000).	To get from hectaliters to centiliters, you must move up four stairs. So, multiply by 10^4 (or 10,000).
5,700 mL ÷ 1,000 = 5.7 L	7.38 hL × 10,000 = 73,800 cL

DIRECTIONS: Use the chart to help you convert the metric units.

1. 16 dL = _____ mL

2. 162,100 mL = _____ hL

3. 8.9 daL = _____ dL

4. 16 kL = _____ mL

5. 9 L = _____ hL

6. 16.8 hL = _____ cL

7. 0.06 hL = _____ mL

8. 0.08 L = _____ cL

9. 0.06 daL = _____ cL

DIRECTIONS: Compare the following measurements using <, >, or =.

10. 296 mL _____ 3 L

11. 11.61 hL _____ 11,000 dL

12. 5 kL _____ 5,000 L

STOP

Mathematics

4.A

Mass Measurements–Metric

Measurement

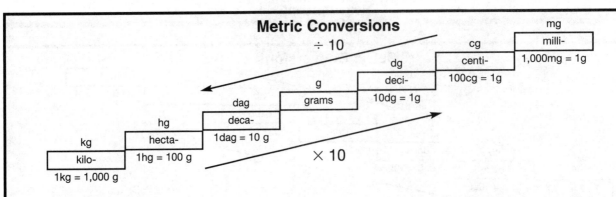

Multiply when moving up on the chart—from kiloliters to liters or from liters to centiliters. Divide when moving down on the chart—from milliliters to deciliters or from meters to hectoliters.

Smaller Units to Larger Units	**Larger Units to Smaller Units**
6,095 mg = _____ g	_____ cg = 7.52 hg
To get from milligrams to grams, you must move down three stairs. So, divide by 10^3 (or 1,000).	To get from hectagrams to centigrams, you must move up four stairs. So, multiply by 10^4 (or 10,000).
6,095 mg ÷ 1,000 = 6.095 g	7.52 hg × 10,000 = 75,200 cg

DIRECTIONS: Use the chart to help you convert the metric units.

1. 7.2 kg = _____ dg

2. 11.01g = _____ mg

3. 16.013 kg = _____ dag

4. 0.062 g = _____ cg

5. 310 hg = _____ g

6. 0.013 cg = _____ hg

7. 21.9 dag = _____ kg

8. 0.121 cg = _____ dg

9. 11.61 hg = _____ dg

DIRECTIONS: Compare the following measurements using <, >, or =.

10. 6.2 kg _____ 5,000 g

11. 12,437 mg _____ 1.2437 dag

12. 79 dg _____ 9 g

STOP

Mathematics

4.B

Determining the Volume of Right Prisms and Cylinders
Measurement

DIRECTIONS: Choose the best answer.

 Clue A **right prism** is a prism in which the top and bottom polygons lie on top of each other so that the vertical polygons connecting their sides are rectangles.

1. Which of the following shapes is a cylinder?

   Ⓐ   Ⓒ

   Ⓑ   Ⓓ

2. Which of the following shapes is a right prism?

   Ⓕ   Ⓗ

   Ⓖ   Ⓙ

3. The formula for the volume of a cylinder is _____ .

   Ⓐ $\pi r^2 \times h$

   Ⓑ $\pi d \times l$

   Ⓒ $\pi b \times h \times l$

   Ⓓ πr^2

4. The formula for the volume of a right prism is _____ .

   Ⓕ $B \times h$

   Ⓖ $\frac{1}{2} b \times h$

   Ⓗ $\frac{1}{2} b \times h \times l$

   Ⓙ s^3

5. Find the volume of a cylinder with radius = 5 and length = 7. Use π = 3.14.

   Ⓐ   109.9 units^3 Ⓒ   175 units^3

   Ⓑ   78.5 units^3 Ⓓ   549.5 units^3

6. What is the volume of a right prism with a length of 8 feet, a height of 6 feet, and a width of 2 feet?

   Ⓕ   16 cubic feet

   Ⓖ   18 cubic feet

   Ⓗ   96 cubic feet

   Ⓙ   32 cubic feet

7. What is the volume of the following right prism?

   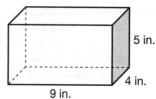

   5 in.
   4 in.
   9 in.

   Ⓐ   18 in.^{3}

   Ⓑ   41 in.^{3}

   Ⓒ   180 in.^{3}

   Ⓓ   90 in.^{3}

8. What is the volume of the following cylinder? Use π = 3.14.

   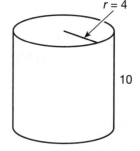

   r = 4
   10

   Ⓕ   62.8 units^3

   Ⓖ   125.6 units^3

   Ⓗ   502.4 units^3

   Ⓙ   251.2 units^3

   STOP

Mathematics

Finding the Surface Area
of Prisms and Cylinders

Measurement

DIRECTIONS: Use the diagram and the net below to answer questions 1–4.

Surface area (SA) is the total area of the faces and curved surfaces of a solid figure. To find the surface area, simply add the area of each face.

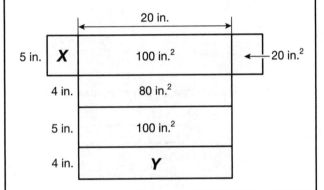

3. **Which of the following formulas shows how to find the surface area of the right prism at the left?**

   Ⓐ   SA = 100 + 80 + 20

   Ⓑ   SA = X + 100 + 80 + 20

   Ⓒ   SA = X + Y + 100 + 80 + 20

   Ⓓ   SA = X + Y + 100 + 100 + 20 + 80

4. **What is the surface area of this right prism?**

   Ⓕ   200 in.^{2}

   Ⓖ   400 in.^{2}

   Ⓗ   600 in.^{2}

   Ⓙ   800 in.^{2}

DIRECTIONS: Use the diagram below to answer question 5.

The formula for finding the surface area of a cylinder is $2\pi rh + 2B$.

B is the area of the base, so $B = \pi r^2$.

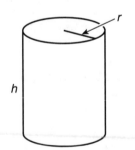

1. **What is the area of side X?**

   Ⓐ   20 in.^{2}

   Ⓑ   40 in.^{2}

   Ⓒ   45 in.^{2}

   Ⓓ   100 in.^{2}

2. **What is the area of side Y?**

   Ⓕ   20 in.^{2}

   Ⓖ   40 in.^{2}

   Ⓗ   80 in.^{2}

   Ⓙ   100 in.^{2}

5. **What is the formula for finding the surface area of a cylinder with a height of 10 and a radius of 5?**

   Ⓐ   SA = $2\pi5(10) + 2(\pi5^2)$

   Ⓑ   SA = $2\pi5(10) + 2(5)$

   Ⓒ   SA = $2\pi5(10) + 2(10)$

   Ⓓ   SA = $2\pi10 + 2(\pi5^2)$

STOP

Mathematics

3.0–4.0

For pages 56–64

Geometry; Measurement

DIRECTIONS: Use the grid for questions 1 and 2.

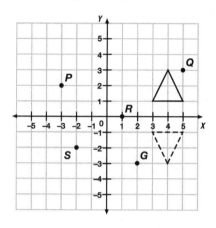

1. Which point is located at (5, 3)?

- (A) R
- (B) G
- (C) Q
- (D) P

2. What type of transformation of the image was performed?

- (F) Reflection across *y*-axis
- (G) Reflection across *x*-axis
- (H) Translation 2 units down
- (J) Translation 6 units down

DIRECTIONS: Choose the best answer.

3. Which of these represents the greatest mass?

- (A) 1.5 grams
- (B) 100 grams
- (C) 4.5 kilograms
- (D) 6 kilograms

4. Which statement about this triangle is true?

- (F) Only one of the angles is an acute angle.
- (G) Two of the angles are obtuse angles.
- (H) There is one right and one acute angle.
- (J) None of the angles are right angles.

5. What is the surface area of a rectangular prism with a length of 6 feet, a height of 4 feet, and a width of 3 feet?

- (A) 54 ft.^{2}
- (B) 96 ft.^{2}
- (C) 108 ft.^{2}
- (D) 120 ft.^{2}

6. Find the volume of a cylinder with a radius of 2 and a length of 9.

- (F) 28.26 units^3
- (G) 113.04 units^3
- (H) 56.52 units^3
- (J) 254.34 units^3

7. How many interior triangles are in a pentagon?

- (A) 2
- (B) 3
- (C) 5
- (D) 10

STOP

Mathematics

5.A

Using Line Graphs and Scatter Plots

Data Analysis and Probability

DIRECTIONS: The graph below shows the basketball game attendance for the season. Use the graph to answer questions 1–3.

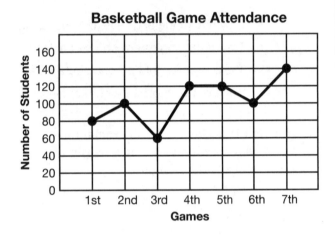

Basketball Game Attendance

1. **What was the increase in attendance from the first to the seventh game?**

   (A)   50 students

   (B)   60 students

   (C)   140 students

   (D)   70 students

2. **Between which two games was there the smallest increase in attendance?**

   (F)   1st and 2nd games

   (G)   6th and 7th games

   (H)   5th and 6th games

   (J)   2nd and 3rd games

3. **What was the average attendance during the season?**

   (A)   about 80

   (B)   about 100

   (C)   about 120

   (D)   about 140

DIRECTIONS: Study the graph below and then answer numbers 4–6.

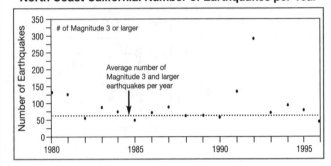

North Coast California: Number of Earthquakes per Year

4. **In what year did the greatest number of earthquakes occur?**

   (F)   1990

   (G)   1991

   (H)   1992

   (J)   1993

5. **In what year did the fewest number of earthquakes occur?**

   (A)   1981

   (B)   1986

   (C)   1991

   (D)   1996

6. **Based on the data, what is an average number of earthquakes per year on the north coast of California?**

   (F)   about 250

   (G)   about 150

   (H)   about 100

   (J)   about 50

STOP

Name _____   Date _____

Mathematics

Mean, Median, Mode, Range, and Quartiles

Data Analysis and Probability

 **Clue** The **mean** of a set of data is the sum of the data divided by the number of pieces of data (average); the **mode** of a set of data is the one that occurs most often; the **median** of a set of data is the number in the middle when the numbers are put in order; the **range** of a set of data is the difference between the greatest value and lowest value of the set; the **upper quartile** is the median of the upper half of the data and the **lower quartile** is the median of the lower half of the data.

DIRECTIONS: Use this data set to answer questions 1–4: 8, 5, 8, 8, 10, 13, 17, 17, 25, 20, 7, 9.

1. What is the mean of the data?
- Ⓐ 8
- Ⓑ 9.5
- Ⓒ 12.25
- Ⓓ 20

2. What is the median of the data?
- Ⓕ 8
- Ⓖ 9.5
- Ⓗ 12.25
- Ⓙ 20

3. What is the mode of the data?
- Ⓐ 8
- Ⓑ 9.5
- Ⓒ 12.25
- Ⓓ 20

4. What are the upper and lower quartiles of the data?
- Ⓕ 17 and 8
- Ⓖ 25 and 5
- Ⓗ 20 and 9
- Ⓙ 25 and 20

DIRECTIONS: Use this data set for questions 5–8.

The basketball attendance per game for the season was: 80, 100, 60, 120, 120, 100, 140.

5. What is the range of the data?
- Ⓐ 80
- Ⓑ 100
- Ⓒ 100, 120
- Ⓓ 102.9

6. What is the mean of the data?
- Ⓕ 80
- Ⓖ 100
- Ⓗ 100, 120
- Ⓙ 102.9

7. What is the median of the data?
- Ⓐ 80
- Ⓑ 100
- Ⓒ 100, 120
- Ⓓ 102.9

8. What is the mode of the data?
- Ⓕ 80
- Ⓖ 100
- Ⓗ 100, 120
- Ⓙ 102.9

STOP

Name _____ Date _____

 5.C

Using Samples

Data Analysis and Probability

DIRECTIONS: Explain your answers in complete sentences.

Clue — Read each problem carefully and make sure you understand what is being asked.

1. In a random sample of 35 students in the school cafeteria, Marsha found that 15 ordered spaghetti. If there are 525 students who eat the cafeteria lunch, how many will likely order spaghetti?

_____

_____

_____

2. Is the sample in question 1 a good sampling of the population? Explain.

_____

_____

3. Why might you choose to use the sample survey rather than survey the entire population? Explain.

_____

_____

_____

4. Mickey took a survey of sweatshirt sizes from a random sample of 25 students. The shirts are to be sold in a bookstore at a school with 950 students. Should the sample be larger? Explain.

_____

_____

5. A pre-election poll predicted that a certain candidate for the school board would receive 30% of the vote. She actually received 10,921 votes. Estimate how many people voted in the election if the poll was a good prediction.

_____

_____

_____

_____

6. A pre-election poll predicted that a certain candidate for county treasurer would receive 25% of the vote. He actually received 75%. Was this poll useful? Explain.

_____

_____

_____

_____

7. Give two reasons why the pre-election poll could have been so far off in question 6.

_____

_____

_____

_____

Mathematics

5.D

Determining Probability
Given Possible Outcomes
Data Analysis and Probability

DIRECTIONS: Choose the best answer. Choose "not given" only if you are sure the right answer is not one of the choices.

 Clue Look for key words, numbers, and figures in each problem, and be sure you perform the correct operation.

1. **There are 10 silver earrings and 10 gold earrings in a drawer. Cheryl reaches into her jewelry box without looking. What is the probability that she will pick a gold earring?**

   Ⓐ $\frac{1}{2}$ Ⓒ $\frac{1}{4}$

   Ⓑ $\frac{1}{3}$ Ⓓ not given

2. **A group of teachers are ordering sandwiches from the deli. They can choose ham, beef, turkey, or bologna on white bread, wheat bread, or rye bread. How many different meat and bread combinations are possible?**

   Ⓕ 12
   Ⓖ 16
   Ⓗ 7
   Ⓙ not given

3. **Elliott spun the arrow on a spinner 30 times. The results are shown in the table. Which of these spinners did Elliott most likely spin?**

Diamond	Heart	Spade	Total Spins
11	10	9	30

   Ⓐ   Ⓑ   Ⓒ   Ⓓ

4. **A snack food company makes chewy fruit shapes of lions, monkeys, elephants, and giraffes in red, green, purple, and yellow. They put the same number of each kind in a package. How many different outcomes are there?**

   Ⓕ 4
   Ⓖ 8
   Ⓗ 16
   Ⓙ not given

DIRECTIONS: For questions 5 and 6, draw a tree diagram to show all the outcomes.

5. **Draw the diagram for question 2.**

6. **A new car can be ordered in black, red, or tan. You may also choose leather or fabric seats. Show the outcomes.**

STOP

Mathematics

6.A

Solving Problems
Process

DIRECTIONS: Choose the best answer.

1. Monica spent $\frac{1}{3}$ hour folding her laundry and $\frac{3}{4}$ hour cleaning her room. Which equation shows how much time she spent doing her housework?

   (A) $\frac{1}{3} \times \frac{3}{4} = t$

   (B) $\frac{3}{4} \div \frac{1}{3} = t$

   (C) $\frac{1}{3} + \frac{3}{4} = t$

   (D) $\frac{1}{3} - \frac{3}{4} = t$

2. Every Monday, Max works 8 hours at the widget factory, where he assembles an average of 30 widgets each hour. Which equation shows how many widgets Max assembles on a typical Monday?

   (F) $8 \times 24 = w$

   (G) $8 + 30 = w$

   (H) $8 \times 30 = w$

   (J) $24 \div 8 = w$

3. Suppose 240 people attend Friday night's football game between the Central High Giants and the St. Mary's Falcons. If $\frac{3}{5}$ of the crowd are Falcon's fans, which equation shows how many are Giants fans?

   (A) $240 - (240 \times \frac{2}{5}) = f$

   (B) $240 \times \frac{3}{5} = f$

   (C) $240 \div \frac{2}{5} = f$

   (D) $240 \times \frac{2}{5} = f$

4. Bethany is helping her grandpa put new tile down on the kitchen floor. The floor surface measures 14 feet wide by 18 feet long. The tiles they are using can cover an area of 2 square feet each. Which of these shows how many tiles they will need to cover the floor surface?

   (F) $(14 \times 18) \div 2 = \blacksquare$

   (G) $(14 \times 18) \times 2 = \blacksquare$

   (H) $14 + 18 + 2 = \blacksquare$

   (J) $(14 \div 2) \times 12 = \blacksquare$

DIRECTIONS: For questions 5–6, imagine that the temperature in Siler City at 7:00 A.M. was −5°F. By 12:00 noon, the temperature increased to 15°F, but it fell by 3°F by 6:00 P.M.

5. How much did the temperature increase between 7:00 A.M. and 12:00 noon?

   (A) −5°F

   (B) −20°F

   (C) 5°F

   (D) 20°F

6. What is the average hourly temperature gain between 7:00 A.M. and 12:00 noon?

   (F) −4°F

   (G) 20°F

   (H) 4°F

   (J) −20°F

STOP

Mathematics

6.B/6.C

Evaluating Mathematical Arguments

Process

DIRECTIONS: Choose the best answer.

1. **Which of these statements is true?**

   (A) When a whole number is multiplied by 3, the product will always be an odd number.

   (B) When a whole number is multiplied by 4, the product will always be an even number.

   (C) All numbers that can be divided by 5 are odd numbers.

   (D) The product of an odd and even number is always an odd number.

2. **Betsy has 7 quarters, 8 nickels, 9 dimes, 67 pennies, and 3 half-dollars. How much money does she have altogether?**

   (F) $8.43

   (G) $5.22

   (H) $7.32

   (J) $6.22

3. **The area of Mr. White's classroom is 981.75 square feet. The gym is 4.5 times as large. What is the area of the gym?**

   (A) 4,500.12 square feet

   (B) 4,417.875 square feet

   (C) 986.25 square feet

   (D) 4,411.78 square feet

4. **Which of these statements is true?**

   (F) 11 quarters is worth more than 19 dimes.

   (G) 50 nickels is worth more than 25 dimes.

   (H) 6 quarters is worth more than 16 dimes.

   (J) 15 nickels is worth more than 9 dimes.

5. **Sven went grocery shopping with his mother. The groceries totaled $36.37. Sven's mom paid for the food with two $20 bills. Which of these is the correct amount of change she should receive?**

   (A) 2 one-dollar bills, two quarters, two dimes, and three pennies

   (B) 3 one-dollar bills, two quarters, one dime, and three pennies

   (C) 3 one-dollar bills, three quarters, one nickel, and three pennies

   (D) none of these

6. **What should replace the box in the number sentence below?**

   $$8 \times 7 = (6 \times 6) + (4 \times \blacksquare)$$

   (F) 4

   (G) 6

   (H) 5

   (J) 7

7. **The guidebook for the Boardwalk has a star that extends from the front cover to the back cover. How many points are on the star when the book is open?**

   (A) 5 points

   (B) 6 points

   (C) 7 points

   (D) 8 points

Welcome to the Boardwalk!

STOP

Mathematics

6.D

Applying Math to Other Areas

Process

DIRECTIONS: Choose the best answer.

Recently, 250 seventh-graders were asked which type of movie is their favorite. The graph below shows the percentage of students who liked each type of movie the best. Use it to answer questions 1 and 2.

1. **Which type of movie did most seventh-graders prefer?**

   (A) action movies

   (B) dramas

   (C) comedies

   (D) romance movies

2. **How many students liked mystery movies the best?**

   (F) 12

   (G) 30

   (H) 50

   (J) 60

Your family wants to plant a new flower garden and you volunteer to do some comparative shopping to find the best deal. Use the information in the chart to answer questions 3 and 4.

	Jenny's Garden Store	**The Flower Shoppe**
Marigolds	1 dozen for $6.50	1 dozen for $7.00
Violets	6 for $3.00	1 dozen for $5.50
Petunias	1 dozen for $4.00	1 dozen for $4.50
Impatiens	1 dozen for $8.00	1 dozen for $15.00

3. **How much would it cost to buy a dozen violets and six impatiens at Jenny's Garden Store?**

   (A) $9.25

   (B) $10.00

   (C) $11.00

   (D) $12.50

4. **How much would it cost to buy a dozen violets and six impatiens at The Flower Shoppe?**

   (F) $13.00

   (G) $10.00

   (H) $11.00

   (J) $12.50

Name _____   Date _____

Communicating Mathematical Ideas
Process

DIRECTIONS: Choose the best answer.

1. What number completes this number sentence?

   $32 \times 7 = 32 \times (\underline{} \div 3)$

   (A) 4

   (B) 7

   (C) 21

   (D) 28

2. What is the perimeter of this parallelogram?

   (F) 88 inches

   (G) 19 inches

   (H) 38 inches

   (J) 28 inches

   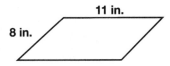

   11 in.

   8 in.

3. Look at the two squares below. What is the area of the shaded portion of the larger square?

   (A) 84 m^2

   (B) 40 m^2

   (C) 116 m^2

   (D) 30 m^2

   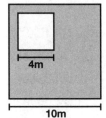

   4m

   10m

4. What is the missing number?

   $\dfrac{9}{11} = \dfrac{\blacksquare}{88}$

   (F) 62

   (G) 11

   (H) 99

   (J) 72

5. Which number represents the total proportion of unshaded figures?

   (A) $\dfrac{1}{2}$

   (B) $\dfrac{7}{16}$

   (C) $\dfrac{8}{16}$

   (D) $\dfrac{1}{4}$

6. About how much will the apples on the scale cost?

   99¢/LB

   39¢/LB

   $1.59/LB

   (F) $1.00

   (G) $3.00

   (H) $4.50

   (J) $7.50

7. Which point is at $\dfrac{1}{2}$ on this number line?

   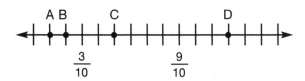

   A B   C   D

   $\dfrac{3}{10}$ $\dfrac{9}{10}$

   (A) A

   (B) B

   (C) C

   (D) D

STOP

Mathematics

| 5.0–6.0 |

For pages 66–73

| **Mini-Test 3** |

Data Analysis and Probability; Process

DIRECTIONS: Choose the best answer.

1. The sweaters on sale come in three styles: pullover, cardigan, and turtleneck. They come in three colors: black, white, and red. How many choices are there?

   Ⓐ 9 choices

   Ⓑ 6 choices

   Ⓒ 3 choices

   Ⓓ 12 choices

2. For question 1, what is the probability of choosing a black pullover?

   Ⓕ $\frac{1}{12}$ Ⓗ $\frac{1}{6}$

   Ⓖ $\frac{1}{9}$ Ⓙ $\frac{1}{3}$

3. Which of these statements is correct?

   Ⓐ 9 quarters is worth more than 12 dimes.

   Ⓑ 12 dimes is worth more than 50 nickels.

   Ⓒ 50 nickels is worth less than 9 quarters.

   Ⓓ 50 nickels is worth less than 12 dimes.

DIRECTIONS: Use this data set for questions 4–5. The test scores for a class are: 86, 94, 70, 81, 92, 74, 75, 89, 76, 97.

4. What is the median of the data?

   Ⓕ 27

   Ⓖ 83.4

   Ⓗ 83.5

   Ⓙ none of the above

5. What is the mean of the data?

   Ⓐ 27

   Ⓑ 83.4

   Ⓒ 83.5

   Ⓓ none of the above

6. The Mathematics Building is 68.3 feet from the Computer Center. The Library is 5 times farther from the Computer Center than the Mathematics Building. What is the distance from the Computer Center to the Library?

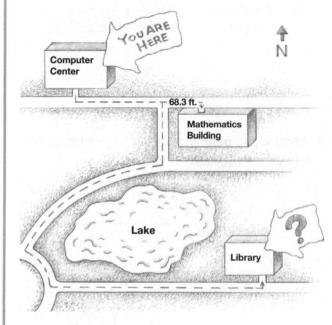

   Ⓕ 3,415.0 feet

   Ⓖ 341.5 feet

   Ⓗ 73.3 feet

   Ⓙ 13.66 feet

7. This graph shows Linda's math average over the course of one semester. About how much did her average increase from September to October?

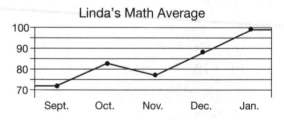

   Ⓐ 5

   Ⓑ 10

   Ⓒ 20

   Ⓓ 30

How Am I Doing?

Mini-Test 1

Page 55

Number Correct

8 answers correct	**Great Job!** Move on to the section test on page 76.
5–7 answers correct	**You're almost there!** But you still need a little practice. Review practice pages 45–54 before moving on to the section test on page 76.
0–4 answers correct	**Oops!** Time to review what you have learned and try again. Review the practice section on pages 45–54. Then, retake the test on page 55. Now, move on to the section test on page 76.

Mini-Test 2

Page 65

Number Correct

7 answers correct	**Awesome!** Move on to the section test on page 76.
4–6 answers correct	**You're almost there!** But you still need a little practice. Review practice pages 56–64 before moving on to the section test on page 76.
0–3 answers correct	**Oops!** Time to review what you have learned and try again. Review the practice section on pages 56–64. Then, retake the test on page 65. Now, move on to the section test on page 76.

Mini-Test 3

Page 74

Number Correct

7 answers correct	**Great Job!** Move on to the section test on page 76.
4–6 answers correct	**You're almost there!** But you still need a little practice. Review practice pages 66–73 before moving on to the section test on page 76.
0–3 answers correct	**Oops!** Time to review what you have learned and try again. Review the practice section on pages 66–73. Then, retake the test on page 74. Now, move on to the section test on page 76.

Final Mathematics Test
for pages 45–73

1. **Identify the property that makes the number sentence $6(7 + n) = 6 \times 7 + 6n$ true.**

   (A) commutative

   (B) distributive

   (C) associative

   (D) both A and B

2. $1\frac{1}{12} \times \frac{3}{8} =$ _____

   (F) $\frac{31}{32}$ (H) $\frac{3}{32}$

   (G) $\frac{1}{4}$ (J) $\frac{13}{32}$

3. $\frac{8}{9} \div \frac{1}{4} =$ _____

   (A) $5\frac{1}{3}$ (C) $3\frac{5}{9}$

   (B) $\frac{1}{36}$ (D) $\frac{2}{9}$

4. **A hiker started out with 48 ounces of water. She drank 9 ounces of water after hiking 5 miles and 16 more ounces when she reached mile marker 8. How many ounces of water did she have left?**

   (F) $48 - (9 + 16) = \blacksquare$

   (G) $48 + (9 - 16) = \blacksquare$

   (H) $(16 - 9) + 48 = \blacksquare$

   (J) $48 + 9 + 16 = \blacksquare$

5. **A sock drawer has 5 brown pairs of socks, 3 red pairs of socks, and 6 blue pairs of socks. Which of the following does not show the ratio of red to blue?**

   (A) $\frac{3}{6}$

   (B) 3:6

   (C) $\frac{1}{3}$

   (D) 3 to 6

6. $\frac{7}{49} = \frac{12}{n}$

   (F) 54

   (G) 144

   (H) 7

   (J) 84

7. **What is the perimeter of a room that measures 11 feet by 15 feet?**

   (A) 16 feet

   (B) 27 feet

   (C) 52 feet

   (D) 165 feet

8. **6 L =** _____

   (F) 60 mL

   (G) 600 mL

   (H) 6,000 mL

   (J) 60,000 mL

9. **75,000 g =** _____

   (A) 7.5 kg

   (B) 75 kg

   (C) 750 kg

   (D) 7,500 kg

10. **Which of the triangles below is acute?**

    (F)   (G)   (H)   (J)

GO

11. Which of the following open sentences has the same solution set as $4a + 3 = 27$?

(A) $3 + a = 15$

(B) $27 - a = 20$

(C) $6 \times a = 36$

(D) $60 \div a = 12$

12. Choose the symbol that would make the following number sentence true.

$$5(6 + 7) \;\square\; 8^2$$

(F) $<$

(G) $>$

(H) $=$

(J) none of the above

13. Jacob has a bag with 13 pieces of candy. His father puts some more candy into the bag. He now has 28 pieces. Which equation shows how many pieces his father gave him?

(A) $28 \div 13 = \blacksquare$

(B) $13 + \blacksquare = 28$

(C) $28 \times 13 = \blacksquare$

(D) $13 - \blacksquare = 28$

14. What is the value of y if $(8 \times y) + 15 = 87$?

(F) 7

(G) 8

(H) 9

(J) 10

15. The Medina Valley daily newspaper costs $0.35 each day, except for the Sunday edition, which costs $1.25. When Bucky's family went on vacation for 2 weeks, they canceled their subscription for the time they were gone. Which expression can be used to determine how much money they saved by canceling their subscription during their vacation?

(A) $7 \times (1.25 + 0.35)$

(B) $(2 \times 1.35) + (2 \times 0.35)$

(C) $(2 \times 7) \times (1.25 + 0.35)$

(D) $(2 \times 6 \times 0.35) + (2 \times 1.25)$

DIRECTIONS: The graph below shows the average number of rainy days per month in Sun City, Florida. Use the graph to answer questions 16–18.

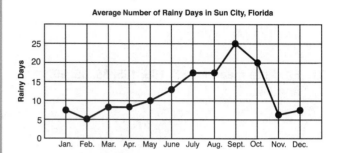

Average Number of Rainy Days in Sun City, Florida

16. Which two-month period shows the greatest change in the number of rainy days?

(F) May and June

(G) June and July

(H) October and November

(J) August and September

17. How many inches of rain fell during the rainiest month?

(A) 20 inches

(B) 25 inches

(C) about 18 inches

(D) none of the above

18. Based on this graph, which two months should have been the best for tourists who do not like rain?

(F) January and February

(G) February and November

(H) March and April

(J) April and December

19. Find the mode for 85, 105, 135, 85, and 65.

(A) 70

(B) 85

(C) 86

(D) 95

GO

20. Find the median for 85, 105, 135, 85, and 65.

(F) 70

(G) 85

(H) 86

(J) 95

21. Find the mean for 85, 105, 135, 85, 65, 80, and 84.

(A) 70

(B) 85

(C) 86

(D) 91.3

22. The convenience store has a choice of chocolate, vanilla, and strawberry frozen yogurt in either a sugar cone or a waffle cone. How many choices are there?

(F) 9

(G) 6

(H) 3

(J) 5

23. For question 22, what is the probability that you will choose a chocolate frozen yogurt on a waffle cone?

(A) $\frac{1}{3}$

(B) $\frac{1}{5}$

(C) $\frac{1}{6}$

(D) $\frac{1}{9}$

24. Hector's neighborhood is having a large garage sale. The expenses are $10 for flyers, $35 for advertising, and $50 for table rentals. They made a total of $525. How much profit did they make?

(F) $620

(G) $430

(H) $525

(J) $95

25. In question 24, there were 5 families taking part in the rummage sale. How much does each family get?

(A) $105

(B) $124

(C) $19

(D) $86

26. A shoe box is 6 inches wide, 11 inches long, and 5 inches high. Find the volume of the box.

(F) 330 cubic inches

(G) 22 cubic inches

(H) 660 cubic inches

(J) 33 cubic inches

27. This table shows the total number of ice pops contained in different numbers of boxes.

Number of Boxes	Number of Ice Pops
2	24
3	36
4	48
5	60

If the pattern continues, which number sentence shows how you could calculate the number of ice pops in 11 boxes?

(A) 60 ÷ 11 = ■

(B) 11 × 12 = ■

(C) 5 × 11 = ■

(D) 12 + 60 = ■

28. Which of these are the coordinates of the triangle?

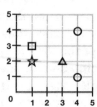

(F) (1, 2)

(G) (3, 2)

(H) (1, 3)

(J) (4, 4)

STOP

Mathematics Test
Answer Sheet

1 Ⓐ Ⓑ Ⓒ Ⓓ
2 Ⓕ Ⓖ Ⓗ Ⓙ
3 Ⓐ Ⓑ Ⓒ Ⓓ
4 Ⓕ Ⓖ Ⓗ Ⓙ
5 Ⓐ Ⓑ Ⓒ Ⓓ
6 Ⓕ Ⓖ Ⓗ Ⓙ
7 Ⓐ Ⓑ Ⓒ Ⓓ
8 Ⓕ Ⓖ Ⓗ Ⓙ
9 Ⓐ Ⓑ Ⓒ Ⓓ
10 Ⓕ Ⓖ Ⓗ Ⓙ

11 Ⓐ Ⓑ Ⓒ Ⓓ
12 Ⓕ Ⓖ Ⓗ Ⓙ
13 Ⓐ Ⓑ Ⓒ Ⓓ
14 Ⓕ Ⓖ Ⓗ Ⓙ
15 Ⓐ Ⓑ Ⓒ Ⓓ
16 Ⓕ Ⓖ Ⓗ Ⓙ
17 Ⓐ Ⓑ Ⓒ Ⓓ
18 Ⓕ Ⓖ Ⓗ Ⓙ
19 Ⓐ Ⓑ Ⓒ Ⓓ
20 Ⓕ Ⓖ Ⓗ Ⓙ

21 Ⓐ Ⓑ Ⓒ Ⓓ
22 Ⓕ Ⓖ Ⓗ Ⓙ
23 Ⓐ Ⓑ Ⓒ Ⓓ
24 Ⓕ Ⓖ Ⓗ Ⓙ
25 Ⓐ Ⓑ Ⓒ Ⓓ
26 Ⓕ Ⓖ Ⓗ Ⓙ
27 Ⓐ Ⓑ Ⓒ Ⓓ
28 Ⓕ Ⓖ Ⓗ Ⓙ

Social Studies Standards

Standard 1—Culture *(See pages 81–83.)*
Social studies programs should include experiences that provide for the study of culture and cultural diversity.

Standard 2—Time, Continuity, and Change *(See pages 84–85.)*
Social studies programs should include experiences that provide for the study of the way human beings view themselves in and over time.

Standard 3—People, Places, and Environments *(See pages 86–87.)*
Social studies programs should include experiences that provide for the study of people, places, and environments.

Standard 4—Individual Development and Identity *(See pages 89–90.)*
Social studies programs should include experiences that provide for the study of individual development and identity.

Standard 5—Individuals, Groups, and Institutions *(See pages 91–92.)*
Social studies programs should include experiences that provide for the study of individuals, groups, and institutions.

Standard 6—Power, Authority, and Governance *(See pages 94–95.)*
Social studies programs should include experiences that provide for the study of how people create and change structures of power, authority, and governance.

Standard 7—Production, Distribution, and Consumption *(See pages 96–98.)*
Social studies programs should include experiences that provide for the study of how people organize for the production, distribution, and consumption of goods and services.

Standard 8—Science, Technology, and Society *(See page 99.)*
Social studies programs should include experiences that provide for the study of relationships among science, technology, and society.

Standard 9—Global Connections *(See pages 101–102.)*
Social studies programs should include experiences that provide for the study of global connections and interdependence.

Standard 10—Civic Ideals and Practices *(See pages 103–104.)*
Social studies programs should include experiences that provide for the study of the ideals, principles, and practices of citizenship in a democratic republic.

Social Studies

| 1.0 |

Comparing Aspects of Different Cultures
Culture

DIRECTIONS: Read through the instructions below and then complete the activity.

Select two of the pairs listed below. Visit the library or go online to find examples of each pair. Then for each pair, write a brief report that (1) tells who created the works and identifies the culture(s) where they originated; (2) describes, compares, and contrasts the works; and (3) describes which you prefer and why. Use a separate sheet of paper if needed.

- Australian Aboriginal folktale/Canadian legend
- Statue of Christ the Redeemer in Rio de Janeiro, Brazil/Eiffel Tower in Paris, France
- John Donne poem/Emily Dickinson poem
- Native Polynesian music/Traditional Andean music
- Aztec art/French Impressionist art
- The Opera House in Sydney, Australia/St. Basil's Cathedral in Moscow, Russia
- Frida Kahlo painting/Jackson Pollock painting
- Stone statues (Moais), Easter Island/Stonehenge, England
- The Parthenon in Athens, Greece/Machu Picchu, in Peru
- Polka music/Salsa music

1. **1st Pair:**

_____

_____

_____

_____

_____

_____

2. **2nd Pair:**

_____

_____

_____

_____

_____

_____

STOP

Name _____   Date _____

Social Studies

Interpreting Situations Differently

Culture

DIRECTIONS: Read the passage below, and then answer the questions that follow.

> Our teacher told us that we could work on the assignment by ourselves, or we could work with a partner. I noticed that Josh was working by himself. Josh is a good student, so I thought he'd make a good partner. I asked him if he'd like to work on the assignment with me. He said he'd think about it.
>
> Josh and I are usually friendly to each other, but I still felt a little uncomfortable. Maybe Josh just wanted to work on the assignment by himself. Maybe he didn't want to work with me but wouldn't mind working with another white student. Or maybe he thought I was trying to show how "open-minded" I was by asking the only black kid in class to be my partner. I couldn't tell what he thought, and it made me feel really self-conscious.

1. **From the narrator's perspective, why did he ask Josh to be his partner?**

   _____

   _____

   _____

2. **According to the narrator, what other reason might Josh think he had for asking him to be his partner?**

   _____

   _____

   _____

3. **What are some other reasons that Josh might not want to be the narrator's partner?**

   _____

   _____

   _____

4. **What do you think is the root problem underlying the awkward situation described by the narrator?**

   _____

   _____

STOP

Spectrum Test Prep Grade 7

Social Studies

| 1.0 |

Transmitting Culture Through Toys
Culture

DIRECTIONS: Read the passage below, and then answer the questions that follow.

> Children have always loved playing with toys. In the American South of the early- and mid-1800s, settlers often made toys for their children out of natural materials, such as wood, corn shucks, cane, apples, and gourds. Dolls often had stuffed cloth bodies and heads made from dried apples or painted hickory nuts. Native Americans shared ways to make corn-shuck dolls with both white and black settlers and made miniatures of their own weapons and tools. "Action" toys were carved from wood and showed everyday activities, such as two men chopping wood or chickens pecking for corn.
>
> Children shot peas or rocks at targets with homemade slingshots. Noisemakers like "the buzzsaw" were also popular. On Sundays in many parts of the South, children could only play with biblically based toys, such as the puzzles Jacob's Ladder and the Pillars of Solomon.

1. **What kinds of materials did Southern settlers use to make toys? Why did they use these materials?**

   _____

   _____

2. **Why were children in the South often allowed to play only with biblically based toys on Sundays? What does this tell us about 19th-century Southern culture?**

   _____

   _____

3. **Based on the passage, what were some kinds of work Southern children saw adults doing? How do you know?**

   _____

   _____

   _____

4. **How do children's toys reflect the culture in which the children live? What do you think future historians will conclude about our own times, based on the things adults give their children to play with?**

   _____

   _____

STOP

Social Studies

2.0

Differences of Historical Opinion

Time, Continuity, and Change

DIRECTIONS: Read the passages below concerning the American Revolution. Then, answer the questions that follow.

Views of a twentieth-century historian:

American colonists had no elected representatives in the British Parliament. Therefore, the British government had no right to tax the colonies. The British tried to raise money in 1765 by requiring a tax stamp on colonial documents, newspapers, and other printed papers. Colonists' opposition to the Stamp Act was justified. Colonists could not be taxed without being represented in Parliament. The Stamp Act obviously weakened the colonists' rights and liberties.

Views of Samuel Johnson, an English writer who lived at the time of the American Revolution:

As man can be in but one place, at once, he cannot have the advantages of multiplied residence. He that will enjoy the brightness of sunshine, must quit the coolness of the shade. He who goes voluntarily to America, cannot complain of losing what he leaves in Europe. He, perhaps, had a right to vote for a knight or burgess; by crossing the Atlantick [sic], he has not nullified [canceled] his right; but he has made its exertion [use] no longer possible. By his own choice he has left a country, where he had a vote and little property, for another, where he has great property, but no vote.

1. **What is the historian's main point?**

   (A) Colonists should never have to pay any taxes of any kind.

   (B) The colonists should not have been taxed because they could not vote in British elections.

   (C) The British had every right to tax their colonies.

   (D) All taxes are unlawful.

2. **What is Samuel Johnson's main point?**

   (F) Whatever the colonists want is acceptable.

   (G) The colonists should be taxed even more heavily.

   (H) Colonists have no right to complain about losing their vote in British elections.

   (J) The British Army should arrest all colonists who refuse to pay their taxes.

3. **What reason does Johnson give to support his position?**

   (A) It is not possible for colonists to vote in British elections because they are too far away.

   (B) The colonists are no better than criminals and do not deserve to vote.

   (C) All colonists are considered property of the British government and have no voting rights.

   (D) Only British citizens can vote in British elections, and the colonists gave up their citizenship when they left England.

Social Studies

| 2.0 |

Using a Chronology
Time, Continuity, and Change

DIRECTIONS: Study the chronology below that includes some key events in the American civil rights movement. Then, answer the questions that follow.

Date	Event
May 1954	In *Oliver Brown et al. v. Board of Education of Topeka, Kansas,* the U.S. Supreme Court rules that segregated schools are unconstitutional.
December 1955	Rosa Parks is arrested in Montgomery, Alabama, for violating segregation laws on a city bus. A black boycott of Montgomery buses begins, lasting about one year.
February 1956	Autherine Lucy is the first black student to attend the University of Alabama.
September 1957	The Little Rock Nine seek to enter Little Rock Central High School but are kept out by rioting whites. President Dwight D. Eisenhower sends in the National Guard to enforce the school's integration.
February 1960	Four black college students ask for service at a whites-only Woolworth's lunch counter in Greensboro, N.C., sparking the sit-in movement.
May 1961	The first Freedom Riders leave Washington, D.C., aboard two buses in an attempt to desegregate Southern bus terminals. After many Freedom Riders are beaten by white mobs, they receive National Guard escorts. In Jackson, Mississippi, they are arrested and sent to jail.
September 1962	When James Meredith attempts to become the first black to study at the University of Mississippi, rioting ensues, eventually quashed by federal troops. Meredith attends his first class on October 1.

1. **The chronology shows that civil rights protesters in the 1950s and 1960s were working especially hard for _____ .**

   (A) the right of blacks and whites to marry

   (B) the banning of slavery

   (C) the right of blacks to freely attend school

   (D) the election of a black president

2. **The U.S. Supreme Court ruled that the Montgomery buses had to be integrated, which ended the black boycott. Based on the chronology, when do you think the court made this ruling?**

   (F) November 1956

   (G) May 1954

   (H) January 1956

   (J) February 1960

3. **White students at the University of Alabama rioted in February–March 1956. Based on the chronology, what do you think is the most likely reason?**

   (A) They were protesting the unfair grading system used at the school.

   (B) They were angry that a black student had been admitted to the University of Alabama.

   (C) They were protesting the unequal treatment of their black classmates.

   (D) They were upset that Auburn University had defeated them in basketball that season.

Name _____   Date _____

Using a Climate Map
People, Places, and Environments

DIRECTIONS: Study the map below that shows the climate regions of Norway. Then, answer the questions.

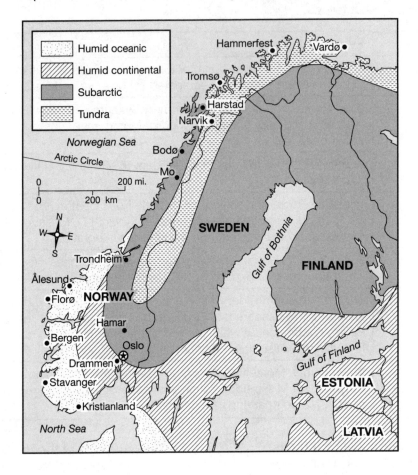

1. **The climate region in the northernmost part of Norway is _____ .**

   (A) subarctic

   (B) humid continental

   (C) tundra

   (D) humid oceanic

2. **Which of the following climate regions in Norway lies entirely south of the Arctic Circle?**

   (F) tundra

   (G) humid continental

   (H) subarctic

   (J) No climate regions in Norway lie south of the Arctic Circle.

3. **Most of the Norwegian cities on this map lie _____ .**

   (A) on the sea

   (B) along the border with Sweden

   (C) in the tundra region

   (D) in the subarctic region

4. **Would you expect the population density in the area surrounding Oslo to be greater or less than in the area surrounding Tromsø? Why?**

   _____

   _____

   _____

STOP

Social Studies

[3.0]

How Human Actions Impact the Environment

People, Places, and Environments

DIRECTIONS: Read the information in the table below. Then, answer the questions that follow.

Region	Environmental Concerns
Canada	• Much of the Pacific rain forest has been clear-cut; the remainder could be gone within 25 years. • Hydroelectric power projects and development in Quebec are disrupting wildlife habitats. • Harvest from commercial fishing in northwest Atlantic has declined over 30% since 1970.
Latin America	• The ecological balance in the Caribbean coral reefs is being upset by a booming tourism industry. • Every year, over 5,000 square miles of rain forest is destroyed in Brazil's Amazon Basin. • Atlantic waters east of Argentina have suffered from overfishing and oil spills.
Europe	• Air pollution and toxic waste dumping in eastern Europe have damaged the environment. • Pollution in the Baltic, Mediterranean, and Black Seas has poisoned the habitat of many local species. • Acid rain, caused by factory emissions, is quickly destroying northern forests.
Oceania	• Overgrazing of livestock in Australia has led to massive desertification and increases the risk of bush fires.

1. **In which region are hydroelectric power projects endangering wildlife habitats?**
   - (A) Guatemala
   - (B) Canada
   - (C) Mexico
   - (D) Cuba

2. **In which region is tourism cited as a main cause of environmental problems?**
   - (F) Oceania
   - (G) the Amazon Basin
   - (H) the northwest Atlantic
   - (J) the Caribbean

3. **At the current rate, how much of the rain forest in Brazil's Amazon Basin will be lost within the next five years?**
   - (A) 5,000 square miles
   - (B) 10,000 square miles
   - (C) 25,000 square miles
   - (D) 50,000 square miles

4. **Overgrazing of livestock has created severe environmental problems in _____ .**
   - (F) the Mediterranean region of Europe
   - (G) northern Canada
   - (H) Australia
   - (J) the Amazon Basin

STOP

Social Studies

1.0–3.0

For pages 81–87

Mini-Test 1

Culture; Time, Continuity, and Change;
People, Places, and Environments

DIRECTIONS: Read the passage below, and then answer the questions that follow.

The *Pax Romana,* meaning *Roman peace,* covered roughly the first two centuries of Rome's emperors, from the rise of Augustus Caesar in 27 B.C. to the death of Marcus Aurelius in A.D. 180. As Rome conquered regions, it introduced its laws and imposed its rule. The era was a period of relative peace, prosperity, and cultural achievement for Rome. Roads were built throughout the empire, making trade easier. People moved easily within the empire, spreading ideas and knowledge throughout the region.

The lands outside of the Roman Empire did not necessarily enjoy the peace of *Pax Romana.* Although Roman rule was fairly lenient, many people lost their freedoms under the Romans. Thousands of people became slaves, and women had few rights. Even within the empire, not all Romans shared equally in the era's prosperity.

1. **Based on the passage above, what event should be at the end of a chronology for the *Pax Romana?***

   _____

2. **Some historians have called the *Pax Romana* the most favorable time in history for the development and advancement of civilization. Based on the passage above, why might some people disagree with this claim?**

   _____

   _____

   _____

   _____

   _____

   _____

3. **According to a Roman legend, the city of Rome was founded by two brothers, Romulus and Remus. The legend says that the brothers were twins who were the sons of Mars, the god of war, and Rhea Silvia, a beautiful priestess. Why might the Romans have included this information about the brothers in the legend?**

   _____

   _____

   _____

DIRECTIONS: Examine the map below to answer question 4.

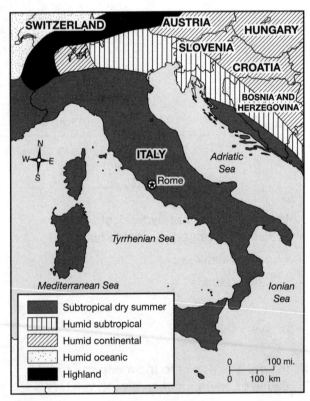

4. **The climate around Rome is _____ .**

   Ⓐ highland

   Ⓑ humid continental

   Ⓒ humid subtropical

   Ⓓ subtropical dry summer

Social Studies

4.0

Stereotyping
Individual Development and Identity

DIRECTIONS: For each of the statements below, write an **S** in the blank if the statement is a stereotype. Write an **N** if the statement is not a stereotype.

 **Clue**

A **stereotype** is an exaggerated image of a particular group. Stereotypes are often based on opinions and distorted ideas and tend not to take into account individual differences among people. A stereotype can be either positive ("Asians are great at math") or negative ("women are more emotional than men"). Whether positive or negative, if a statement about a group of people is broad or oversimplified, it is still a stereotype.

_____ 1. Most kindergarten teachers in the United States are women.

_____ 2. Professional athletes think they're better than everyone else.

_____ 3. Teenage boys drive recklessly.

_____ 4. Most large American corporations are run by men.

_____ 5. Women make better teachers than men.

_____ 6. Poor urban people are more violent than people who live in the suburbs.

_____ 7. College graduates tend to have higher incomes than high school dropouts.

_____ 8. All teenage girls want to do is talk on the phone and shop.

_____ 9. New drivers tend to have more accidents than experienced drivers.

_____ 10. Men are more adventurous than women.

DIRECTIONS: The table below gives examples of images that are often seen in advertisements. For each, describe how the image is a stereotype.

Image	How Is This a Stereotype?
11. Advertisements for food products nearly always show mothers serving meals to their families.	
12. Advertisements often depict teenage girls applying make-up, trying hairstyles, and generally worrying about their appearance. Few show teenage boys doing these things.	
13. Advertisements for action toys, such as trucks and super-hero figures, are targeted almost exclusively to young boys.	STOP

Social Studies

| 4.0 |

Influences on Personality Development
Individual Development and Identity

DIRECTIONS: Read the passage below, and then answer the questions that follow.

> In 1998, Judith Rich Harris wrote a controversial book called *The Nurture Assumption.* In this book, Harris made the claim that the way parents raise their children doesn't have a major effect on the children's personality and behavior. She argued that genetics and relationships with peers have the most impact on children. (*Genetics* refers to traits that are inherited; *peers* refers to friends and schoolmates.)
>
> Harris based many of her theories on studies of adopted children. One large study found that biological children and their parents tested similarly on personality and intelligence tests, while many adopted children and their parents did not. How adoptive parents raised their children didn't seem to have a strong effect on the children's development; genetics appeared to play a much more important role. Harris felt that other studies showed that children are more likely to imitate the behavior of their friends and schoolmates than the behavior of their parents.

1. **According to Harris, what two factors have the strongest effect on children's personality and behavior?**

   _____

   _____

2. **What studies did Harris use to support her theory?**

   _____

   _____

3. **Many studies have shown that parents reading to young children has a strong effect on children's language skills and performance in school. Do these studies support Harris's theory? Explain.**

   _____

   _____

4. **Who do you think has the stronger influence on a child's development—parents or peers? Give two examples to support your answer.**

   _____

   _____

   _____

STOP

Social Studies

| 5.0 |

Marriage in the United States

Individuals, Groups, and Institutions

DIRECTIONS: Read the passage below, and then answer the questions that follow.

Americans have become less likely to marry. From 1970 to 2004, the annual number of marriages among unmarried adult women declined by nearly 50 percent. One reason for this decline is that people are waiting longer to marry. In 1960, the median age at first marriage was 20 for females and 23 for males. By 2004, those ages had risen to 26 and 27, respectively. Nonetheless, since the mid-1800s, about 90 percent of American women have eventually married.

Marriage has many economic benefits. Studies have shown that people who stay married throughout their adult lives tend to be richer than those who divorce or never marry. Yet the number of divorces remains high. The divorce rate in the United States is almost twice what it was in 1960. Since the early 1980s, however, it has been declining slightly. Today, the average recently-married couple has about a 40–50 percent chance of divorcing.

1. **Which of the following statements about marriage is true?**

   Ⓐ Almost all Americans will marry at least once.

   Ⓑ Married couples usually make less money than unmarried people.

   Ⓒ Most Americans marry soon after graduating from high school.

   Ⓓ Fewer than 50 percent of Americans get married.

2. **Divorce in the United States _____ .**

   Ⓕ is against the law in most states

   Ⓖ is a little less common than it was 20 years ago

   Ⓗ was twice as likely to occur in 1960 than it is today

   Ⓙ will affect about 1/4 of all couples

3. **Identify one way American society encourages marriage.**

   _____

   _____

   _____

4. **Identify one way American society discourages divorce.**

   _____

   _____

   _____

5. **About how old are most Americans when they marry for the first time? How does this compare to 40 or 50 years ago? How do you account for this change?**

   _____

   _____

   _____

   _____

   STOP

Social Studies

5.0

Group and Institutional Influences on Society

Individuals, Groups, and Institutions

DIRECTIONS: Read the passage below, and then answer the questions that follow.

> In the United States, the sale of alcoholic beverages became illegal when the Eighteenth Amendment to the Constitution was passed in 1919. Popularly known as *Prohibition,* the passage of the Eighteenth Amendment represented the high point of the American temperance movement. Temperance workers wanted alcohol to be illegal. Some temperance workers wanted this for religious reasons because they thought alcohol use was immoral. Others were opposed to the domestic violence alcohol frequently caused.
>
> From 1920 to 1933, alcoholic beverages were illegal throughout the United States. However, when the Twenty-First Amendment to the Constitution repealed Prohibition, the responsibility for regulating the sale of alcohol was transferred to individual states. Today, most states allow local communities the right to determine how alcohol is sold within their communities.
>
> A *dry county* is a county in the United States where the sale of alcohol is forbidden. There are hundreds of dry counties throughout the U.S., mostly in the South and Midwest. In Texas, for example, 46 counties (out of 254) are totally "dry." Other counties are "moist" (only low-alcohol beverages are legal, or alcohol can be served only at restaurants) or "wet" (all alcohol sales are legal).

1. **One reason temperance workers wanted to make alcoholic beverages illegal was that _____ .**

   (A) they didn't like the way alcohol tasted

   (B) they hated people who drank alcohol

   (C) drinking alcohol was against their religion

   (D) they enjoyed telling people what to do

2. **In the United States today, who decides whether a community is "dry" or "wet"?**

   (F) religious leaders

   (G) voters

   (H) brewers, winemakers, and distillers

   (J) the media

3. **When was Prohibition repealed? Why do you think this happened?**

   _____

   _____

   _____

4. **What kinds of people and institutions do you think have a lot of influence in "dry" counties? Do you think this is different in "wet" counties? Explain your answer.**

   _____

   _____

   _____

   _____

5. **Think of a group of people that has brought about a large change in your community or in American society as a whole. What did they do? What motivated the group?**

   _____

   _____

   _____

   _____

STOP

Social Studies

4.0–5.0

For pages 89–92

Mini-Test 2

**Individual Development and Identity;
Individuals, Groups, and Institutions**

DIRECTIONS: Choose the best answer.

1. **Which of the following is a stereotype?**

   (A) Most Americans speak English.

   (B) Men are better drivers than women.

   (C) Women often make less money than men.

   (D) Women tend to live longer than men.

2. **Which of the following statements about marriage is true?**

   (F) Americans have become less likely to marry.

   (G) Americans are marrying earlier.

   (H) Americans are less likely to divorce today than they were in 1960.

   (J) Single people tend to be richer than married people.

DIRECTIONS: Answer the following questions.

3. **Who do you think has had the greater influence on your development—parents or peers? Explain your answer.**

   _____

   _____

   _____

4. **Think of some characteristic of your community. For example, you may live in a rural area, a small town, a large city, etc. Describe one way your community has affected the kind of person you are.**

   _____

   _____

   _____

5. **For each of the following institutions, list one example of an expected behavior.**

   Family _____

   Marriage _____

   Religion _____

   Schools _____

Social Studies

6.0

Dictatorships and Democracies

Powers, Authority, and Governance

DIRECTIONS: Read the passage below, and then answer the questions that follow.

A *dictatorship* occurs in a nation whose government is completely under the control of a dictator, or all-powerful ruler. The 20th century saw the rise of many dictatorships. Near the end of World War I, Russia became a Communist dictatorship. In 1933, Adolf Hitler set up a dictatorship in Germany. Dictatorships were also set up in Italy, Spain, and most of the Balkan nations. Although dictatorships may include written constitutions and elections, the constitutions do not give freedom to their people, and the government controls the elections. In a dictatorship, people are not allowed to disagree with the government. The idea of individual rights is not valued in a dictatorship. Instead, individuals are valued only to the extent that they can serve the government.

Democracies are the opposite of dictatorships. Democratic government is considered to be the servant of the people, rather than the other way around. Democracies are based on the idea that the people rule. Authority to govern comes from the people. In a democracy, fair and free elections are held regularly. Without an informed and questioning citizenry, a democracy could not survive.

1. **A government that is under the control of an all-powerful ruler is called a _____ .**

   (A) democracy

   (B) dictatorship

   (C) republic

   (D) constitutional monarchy

2. **In a democracy, the authority to rule comes from _____ .**

   (F) the elected officials

   (G) government workers

   (H) the voters

   (J) the Democratic Party

3. **In a dictatorship, who controls the elections?**

   (A) the government

   (B) the president

   (C) the voters

   (D) informed citizenry

4. **In a dictatorship, _____ .**

   (F) free elections are held regularly

   (G) the individual rights of citizens are not valued

   (H) written constitutions are never allowed

   (J) people are allowed to disagree with the government

5. **Why do you think "an informed and questioning citizenry" is essential for a democracy to survive?**

   _____

   _____

   _____

   _____

   _____

STOP

Name _____ Date _____

Social Studies

6.0

The Political System of the United States

Powers, Authority, and Governance

DIRECTIONS: Choose the best answer.

1. **The United States has a form of government that allows its citizens to elect officials to represent them. This form of government is known as _____ .**

   Ⓐ   federalism

   Ⓑ   a dictatorship

   Ⓒ   a monarchy

   Ⓓ   a republic

2. **The Parliament of Canada has two chambers: the House of Commons, which is elected, and the Senate, whose members are appointed by the prime minister. One way this differs from the U.S. Congress is that _____ .**

   Ⓕ   all members of Congress are appointed, not just senators

   Ⓖ   U.S. senators are appointed by the Chief Justice of the Supreme Court

   Ⓗ   the United States has no Senate

   Ⓙ   U.S. senators and representatives are both elected by American citizens

3. **In Argentina, everyone over age 18 is required by law to vote, except for members of the clergy, army personnel, and those deprived for legal reasons. One way this differs from voting requirements in the United States is that _____ .**

   Ⓐ   American citizens can vote when they turn 16

   Ⓑ   American citizens must be at least 30 years old to vote

   Ⓒ   American citizens do not have to vote if they don't want to

   Ⓓ   army personnel are required to vote in the United States

4. **What is the division of governmental powers among the legislative, executive, and judicial branches called?**

   Ⓕ   a constitutional government

   Ⓖ   socialism

   Ⓗ   federalism

   Ⓙ   separation of powers

5. **A system in which each branch of government has some control and influence over the others' power is called _____ .**

   Ⓐ   checks and balances

   Ⓑ   separation of powers

   Ⓒ   democracy

   Ⓓ   federalism

6. **The U.S. Constitution created a federal government that divided the powers between _____ .**

   Ⓕ   national and state governments

   Ⓖ   national and local governments

   Ⓗ   state and local governments

   Ⓙ   national and foreign governments

DIRECTIONS: For each of the positions below, write the name of the person who currently holds that position and indicate if that person is a member of the executive, legislative, or judicial branch of government.

7. **U.S. president:** _____

8. **Chief justice of the U.S. Supreme Court:**

   _____

9. **Congressional representative from your**

   district: _____

10. **One senator from your state:**

    _____   STOP

Name _____ Date _____

Social Studies

Competition, Markets, and Prices

Production, Distribution, and Consumption

DIRECTIONS: Choose the best answer.

1. For years, Phil's Service Station was the only gas station in Smallville. There was no other place to buy gasoline within 30 miles of Phil's. But last week, Biggie Oil Company opened a brand-new gas station about $\frac{1}{4}$ mile from Phil's Service Station. Now that Phil's has a competitor, what do you think will happen to the price of gas at Phil's?

   (A) It will go down.

   (B) It will go up.

   (C) It will stay the same.

   (D) None of the above. Phil's will be out of business within a few days.

2. Consumers decide what to buy because of _____ .

   (F) the quality of a product

   (G) the availability of a product

   (H) the price of a product

   (J) all of the above

3. Suppose you needed some widgets. At what price would you be most likely to purchase the greatest number of them?

   (A) $1.00

   (B) $2.50

   (C) $5.00

   (D) The same number will be purchased no matter the price.

4. When the price of something goes up, the number of people who want to buy the item usually _____ .

   (F) goes up also

   (G) goes down

   (H) stays the same

   (J) drops to zero

5. This fall, Danny decided to charge neighbors $5 per hour to rake leaves. He got a few customers, but not as many as he thought he would. What would most likely happen if Danny lowered his price to $3 per hour?

   (A) More people would decide to let Danny rake their leaves.

   (B) Danny would make a lot less money.

   (C) Danny would lose most of his customers.

   (D) His friend Alison would start raking leaves too at $5 per hour.

6. What happens when supply of a product goes down but demand goes up?

   (F) The price of the product stays the same.

   (G) The price of the product goes down.

   (H) Producers will no longer want to make the product.

   (J) The price of the product goes up.

7. A big winter storm knocked out power to a community for several days. A local store kept several generators in stock. The generators provided a source of electricity. However, the store did not usually sell very many because they were expensive. When the storm hit the community, the store ran out of generators and had to order more. Why do you think people wanted to purchase the generators even though they were still expensive?

   _____

   _____

   _____

   _____

Social Studies

| 7.0 |

The Role of Entrepreneurs

Production, Distribution, and Consumption

DIRECTIONS: Read the story below, and then answer the questions that follow.

> Ten years ago, Wally Anderson opened his own business: Wally's Computer Repair. Wally's business fixes broken computers and printers. Wally used $25,000 of his own money to buy equipment and rent office space. The bank also loaned him $75,000 to help his business get off the ground. (Of course, Wally had to pay the loan back to the bank.)
>
> When Wally first started his store, he was the only employee. He often worked more than 14 hours a day. But over the years, he has hired others to help him with the work. He hired Marcia Fitzgerald to manage the business's finances. Darius Jackson is the lead repair person. Nine other people also work at Wally's store. Wally is very proud of his employees. He is also proud to own his own business. He hopes one day to own and operate another computer repair shop in another town.

 Clue   An **entrepreneur** is someone who starts, runs, and assumes the risk for a business.

1. **In the above story, who is the entrepreneur?**
   - (A) Darius Jackson
   - (B) Marcia Fitzgerald
   - (C) Wally Anderson
   - (D) all of the employees of Wally's Computer Repair

2. **Entrepreneurs _____ .**
   - (F) always make every decision about a business, no matter how small
   - (G) must sometimes borrow money to get their businesses started
   - (H) never hire people to help with their business
   - (J) can own only one business at a time

3. **Wally took some risks when he began his store 10 years ago. Probably the greatest risk he took was that _____ .**
   - (A) he should not have worked 14-hour days
   - (B) he would have lost a lot of money if his business had failed
   - (C) no one should ever try to operate a business alone
   - (D) he did not know how to fix computers

4. **Which of the following statements is not true?**
   - (F) Wally invested a lot of time and money to start his business.
   - (G) Because of Wally, several people have jobs.
   - (H) Ten years ago, Wally did not know for sure if his business would succeed.
   - (J) Now that Wally's business has been around for 10 years, Wally no longer has any risk in running his store.

STOP

Social Studies

| 7.0 |

Banks and
Private Business

Production, Distribution, and Consumption

DIRECTIONS: Study the flowchart below. Then, answer the questions that follow.

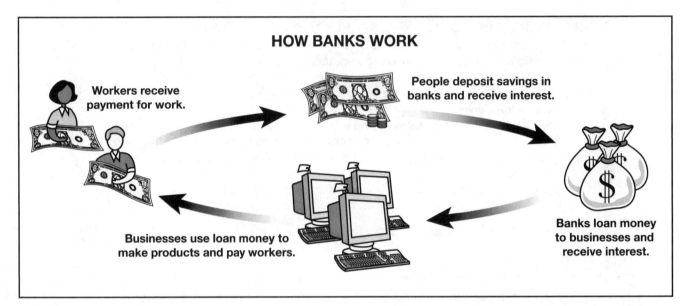

HOW BANKS WORK

Workers receive payment for work.

People deposit savings in banks and receive interest.

Banks loan money to businesses and receive interest.

Businesses use loan money to make products and pay workers.

1. **Why do people deposit money in savings accounts in banks?**

   Ⓐ to receive payment for work

   Ⓑ to make products

   Ⓒ to pay workers

   Ⓓ to receive interest

2. **Why do businesses borrow money?**

   Ⓕ to receive interest

   Ⓖ to make products

   Ⓗ to pay workers

   Ⓙ both G and H

3. **Why do banks loan money?**

   Ⓐ to receive interest

   Ⓑ to make products

   Ⓒ to pay workers

   Ⓓ both B and C

4. **Marcus manages an automobile factory. If he lives in a country that has a market economy, he will determine how many cars he should build this month by _____ .**

   Ⓕ asking the factory employees

   Ⓖ examining the sales figures for the company

   Ⓗ flipping a coin

   Ⓙ none of the above

5. **Suppose you ran a widget factory. As the producer, at what price would you be most likely to produce the greatest number of widgets?**

   Ⓐ $1.00

   Ⓑ $2.50

   Ⓒ $5.00

   Ⓓ the same number no matter what the price

Social Studies

| 8.0 |

Regulation of the
Motion Picture Industry

Science, Technology, and Society

DIRECTIONS: Read the passage below, and then answer the questions that follow.

> All American movies produced during the Great Depression needed to submit to a series of guidelines known as the Motion Picture Production Code, which was established in 1930 by the Motion Picture Producers and Distributors of America. The following are some actual regulations found in the Code:
>
> - Theft, robbery, safe-cracking, and dynamiting of trains, mines, buildings, etc., should not be detailed in method.
> - No film or episode may throw ridicule on any religious faith.
> - Dancing or costumes intended to permit undue exposure or indecent movements in the dance are forbidden.
> - The use of liquor in American life, when not required by the plot or for proper characterization, will not be shown.
> - Excessive and lustful kissing, lustful embraces, and suggestive postures and gestures, are not to be shown.
> - The technique of murder must be presented in a way that will not inspire imitation.
>
> - Obscenity in word, gesture, reference, song, joke, or by suggestion (even when likely to be understood only by part of the audience) is forbidden.
> - Undressing scenes should be avoided, and never used save where essential to the plot.
> - Scenes of actual childbirth, in fact or in silhouette, are never to be presented.
> - Ministers of religion in their character as ministers of religion should not be used as comic characters or as villains.
> - Complete nudity is never permitted.
> - Illegal drug traffic must never be presented.
> - The treatment of bedrooms must be governed by good taste and delicacy.

1. **What do these regulations indicate about the importance of religion and morality in American society during the Great Depression?**

   _____

   _____

   _____

2. **What concern about motion pictures and their influence do these regulations show?**

   _____

   _____

   _____

STOP

Social Studies

6.0–8.0

For pages 94–99

Mini-Test 3

Powers, Authority, and Governance; Production, Distribution, and Consumption; Science, Technology, and Society

DIRECTIONS: Choose the best answer.

1. **Which of the following is true in a dictatorship?**

   Ⓐ The government is completely under the control of an all-powerful ruler.

   Ⓑ The government is considered to be the servant of the people.

   Ⓒ Authority to govern comes from the people.

   Ⓓ Fair and free elections are held regularly.

2. **In the United States, the legislative branch of government is responsible for _____ .**

   Ⓕ interpreting laws

   Ⓖ making laws

   Ⓗ enforcing laws

   Ⓙ all of the above

3. **In a banking system, interest is _____ .**

   Ⓐ earned by the bank

   Ⓑ earned by depositors

   Ⓒ paid by borrowers

   Ⓓ all of the above

4. **Which of the following is most likely to cause the demand for a product to go up?**

   Ⓕ the price goes up

   Ⓖ the producer makes more of the product

   Ⓗ the price goes down

   Ⓙ a rise in unemployment

5. **Francie owns and operates Francie's Corner Deli. Because she runs her own business, we would call her a(n) _____ .**

   Ⓐ competitor

   Ⓑ entrepreneur

   Ⓒ socialist

   Ⓓ unemployed person

DIRECTIONS: Read the passage below and then answer question 6.

Last holiday season, Ziffle's Department Store had 100 Dancing Danny dolls in stock. Dancing Danny dolls were in high demand last year. Ziffle's was able to charge customers $50 each for the dolls and sold them out in one day. This holiday season, Ziffle's ordered 500 of the dolls. Sadly, the Dancing Danny fad has passed. Very few people want the dolls this year.

6. **Which of the following will Ziffle's most likely charge for Dancing Danny dolls this year?**

   Ⓕ $100

   Ⓖ $75

   Ⓗ $50

   Ⓙ $25

DIRECTIONS: Answer the following question.

7. **In the 1930s, when movies were new, they came into conflict with the social values of the time. Give an example of how technology causes conflict with social values today.**

   _____

   _____

   _____

   _____

   _____

STOP

Social Studies

9.0

The Organization of American States

Global Connections

DIRECTIONS: Read the passage below and then answer the questions that follow.

The Organization of American States (OAS) is the oldest regional organization in the world. It brings together most of the nations that make up North and South America. Today, it has 35 member nations. The goal of the OAS is to have peace and justice, to promote unity, and to defend the power, territory, and independence of each member nation.

The idea of creating an organization that united the republics in the Americas started with Simón Bolivar. Bolivar is known for freeing South America from European rule. At the Congress of Panama in 1826, he suggested creating a league of American nations that would work together to defend and govern themselves. This did not come about until much later. In 1890, an international organization was created and, in 1910, it became known as the Pan-American Union. On April 30, 1948, the United States and 20 Latin American republics signed the Charter establishing the Organization of American States in Bogotá, Colombia.

The OAS has been involved with handling conflicts between its member nations. A continuing problem for the OAS has been its relationship with Cuba since the Cuban Revolution in 1959. At that time, Fidel Castro became the new dictator in Cuba. In 1962, Cuba was expelled from the organization on charges of rebellion. Two years later, a trade boycott was placed on Cuba. Nations that were members of the OAS were not to have trade relations with Cuba. By the 1990s, however, practically all member nations except the United States had resumed trade and diplomatic relations with Cuba.

1. **Which of the following is not a goal of the Organization of American States?**

   Ⓐ to have peace and justice

   Ⓑ to promote trade with Europe

   Ⓒ to promote unity

   Ⓓ to defend the power, territory, and independence of each member nation

2. **Which of these events happened first?**

   Ⓕ The Charter establishing the OAS is signed.

   Ⓖ A trade boycott is placed on Cuba.

   Ⓗ The Congress of Panama is held.

   Ⓙ The Pan-American Union is created.

3. **Which of the following countries is not a member of the Organization of American States?**

   Ⓐ Argentina

   Ⓑ Canada

   Ⓒ Mexico

   Ⓓ France

4. **Which nation was expelled from the OAS?**

   Ⓕ Colombia

   Ⓖ United States

   Ⓗ Panama

   Ⓙ Cuba

STOP

Social Studies

| 9.0 |

Contemporary Global Issues
Global Connections

DIRECTIONS: Choose the best answer.

1. **Which of the following is a major cause of world poverty?**

   (A) natural disasters and disease

   (B) people in poor countries having fewer children

   (C) the continuing spread of communism

   (D) wealthy nations' unwillingness to trade with poorer countries

2. **Which of the following statements about human rights around the world is true?**

   (F) Slavery has become a thing of the past.

   (G) Every nation in the world has laws that forbid young children from working.

   (H) People are not jailed today because of their political beliefs.

   (J) Most countries allow women to vote and hold elected office.

3. **A type of pollution in which poisonous chemicals fall back to Earth as precipitation is called _____ .**

   (A) acid rain

   (B) erosion

   (C) poison fog

   (D) ozone depletion

4. **Which of the following organizations has been linked to the 9/11 terrorist attacks against the United States?**

   (F) People for the Ethical Treatment of Animals

   (G) Irish Republican Army

   (H) al-Qaeda

   (J) Palestine Liberation Organization

5. **Global trade tends to _____ .**

   (A) make countries less dependent on each other

   (B) reduce the numbers of products on store shelves

   (C) promote democracy

   (D) make products more expensive

6. **Which of the following statements about the current economic status of women is true?**

   (F) Women own and operate about 90 percent of the world's companies.

   (G) Women own less than 1 percent of world property.

   (H) About 25 percent of the world's women work outside the home.

   (J) Women and men are generally paid the same around the world.

7. **The Kyoto Protocol is an international treaty dealing with _____ .**

   (A) terrorism

   (B) global warming

   (C) voting rights

   (D) genetic engineering

8. **Biological weapons would be most likely to carry _____ .**

   (F) acid rain

   (G) smallpox

   (H) a nuclear warhead

   (J) napalm

STOP

Name _____ Date _____

Writing a Letter
to the Editor
Civic Ideals and Practices

DIRECTIONS: Write a letter to the editor about an issue of your choice. Use the following steps to prepare your letter.

Good citizens stay informed about current issues and discuss important issues with others. One way to contribute to such a discussion in your community is to write a letter to the editor of your local newspaper. In a **letter to the editor,** you defend or promote a certain point of view. If the editor thinks your letter is good, it will be published for other people in your community to read and think about.

1. **Pick a topic that you feel passionate about. If possible, relate it to something discussed in a recent story, editorial, or letter in the newspaper. (Identify the story or letter by its headline and the date it was published.)**

2. **Think of new ways to discuss the topic or new solutions to the problem. Make notes on the lines below.**

_____

_____

_____

_____

3. **Write a first draft of your letter on a separate sheet of paper. Present your views clearly and concisely. Keep your letter short—no more than 250 words. Include your major point in the first paragraph.**

   • If you are responding to an editorial or column, don't attack the writer—focus on his or her views. Offer your own opinion. Address important facts that were ignored. Try to move the debate forward so that other readers might join in the discussion with follow-up letters.

   • If you have read a news story or feature article that relates to something you've experienced, respond by putting your own personal twist on the subject.

4. **Trade letters with a classmate and critique each other's letters.**

5. **Prepare your final draft. If possible, type your letter and double space between lines. Use your spell checker and then proofread.**

6. **Sign your name and include your phone number and address.**

7. **Mail your letter to the address listed for the publication.**

Social Studies

10.0

Rights and Responsibilities of Citizens

Civic Ideals and Practices

DIRECTIONS: Choose the best answer.

1. **The Fifth Amendment to the Constitution protects citizens against incriminating themselves in court. This means that _____ .**

   (A) the judge cannot ask you any questions if you are on trial

   (B) if you have been found innocent of a crime, you can't be tried again for the same crime

   (C) you don't have to give evidence against yourself in court

   (D) you have the right to an attorney to represent you in court

2. **"Because a fighting force of citizens might be necessary to protect a free state, states have the right to allow people to keep weapons in their homes." This is a good summary of which constitutional amendment?**

   (F) First Amendment

   (G) Second Amendment

   (H) Third Amendment

   (J) Fourth Amendment

3. **The Eighth Amendment to the Constitution prohibits unfair punishment. Under the Eighth Amendment, _____ .**

   (A) no one may be imprisoned longer than 20 years

   (B) judges are not allowed to fine lawbreakers

   (C) capital punishment is illegal

   (D) people arrested on a charge can be free while they wait for their trial, if they pay bail money to the court

4. **The Ninth Amendment says _____ .**

   (F) that the only rights a person has are those listed in the Bill of Rights

   (G) that the Bill of Rights does not list all the rights a person has

   (H) that people have only ten rights

   (J) nothing about people's rights

5. **Which of the following is not guaranteed by the Bill of Rights?**

   (A) People have the right to receive basic health care when they are sick, and the government will pay for it.

   (B) People don't have to allow soldiers to stay in their homes during peacetime, nor in time of war unless the government makes a special rule.

   (C) People have the right to freedom of speech, freedom of the press, and freedom of religion.

   (D) Unless there is good reason, the police cannot search people or take their property.

6. **In typical elections, fewer than half of the eligible voters in the United States actually cast a ballot. Some countries fine citizens who do not vote. Would you favor such a law in the United States? Why or why not?**

   _____

   _____

   _____

   _____

   _____

STOP

Social Studies

| 9.0–10.0 |

For pages 101–104

Mini-Test 4

Global Connections; Civic Ideas and Practices

DIRECTIONS: Choose the best answer.

1. **Every right has an accompanying responsibility. For example, all Americans over the age of 18 have the right to vote. But this right means that voters must also** _____ .

   (A) know where the candidates stand on important issues

   (B) attend at least two political speeches every year

   (C) vote for candidates in the same political party each time

   (D) re-elect all current officeholders

2. **To be good citizens in a democracy, people should do all of the following except** _____ .

   (F) keep up on current events

   (G) vote regularly

   (H) agree with the president at all times

   (J) pay taxes

3. **What is acid rain?**

   (A) a gradual increase in the temperature of Earth's atmosphere, caused by industrial pollution and the burning of fossil fuels

   (B) a type of pollution in which poisonous chemicals fall back to Earth as precipitation

   (C) a combination of chemicals that cause ozone depletion

   (D) an illegal drug smuggled from South America

DIRECTIONS: Read the passage below and then answer questions 4–7.

The European Union, or EU, is an economic and political alliance of some European nations. It is responsible for developing a common foreign and security policy for those nations, and for cooperating in justice and home affairs. Perhaps the most important activities of the EU are the promotion of trade among its members, the adoption of a common currency (the euro), and the creation of a central European bank.

4. **What responsibilities do the European Union member nations share?**

   (F) developing a common foreign and security policy

   (G) cooperating in justice and home affairs

   (H) promoting trade among its members

   (J) all of the above

5. **What is the common currency of the European Union?**

   (A) pesetas   (C) euros

   (B) liras   (D) francs

6. **Which of the following nations is not a member of the European Union?**

   (F) France   (H) Germany

   (G) Italy   (J) Kenya

7. **In which way are the European Union and the Organization of American States similar?**

   (A) They have many of the same member nations.

   (B) They are both regional organizations that care about the security of their member nations.

   (C) Neither organization cares about trade issues.

   (D) Neither organization includes the United States.

STOP

How Am I Doing?

Mini-Test 1	4 answers correct	**Great Job!** Move on to the section test on page 108.
Page 88 Number Correct	3 answers correct	**You're almost there!** But you still need a little practice. Review practice pages 81–87 before moving on to the section test on page 108.
	0–2 answers correct	**Oops!** Time to review what you have learned and try again. Review the practice section on pages 81–87. Then, retake the test on page 88. Now, move on to the section test on page 108.
Mini-Test 2	5 answers correct	**Awesome!** Move on to the section test on page 108.
Page 93 Number Correct	4 answers correct	**You're almost there!** But you still need a little practice. Review practice pages 89–92 before moving on to the section test on page 108.
	0–3 answers correct	**Oops!** Time to review what you have learned and try again. Review the practice section on pages 89–92. Then, retake the test on page 93. Now, move on to the section test on page 108.
Mini-Test 3	7 answers correct	**Great Job!** Move on to the section test on page 108.
Page 100 Number Correct	5–6 answers correct	**You're almost there!** But you still need a little practice. Review practice pages 94–99 before moving on to the section test on page 108.
	0–4 answers correct	**Oops!** Time to review what you have learned and try again. Review the practice section on pages 94–99. Then, retake the test on page 100. Now, move on to the section test on page 108.

How Am I Doing?

Mini-Test 4	7 answers correct	**Super!** Move on to the section test on page 108.
Page 105 **Number Correct**	5–6 answers correct	**You're almost there!** But you still need a little practice. Review practice pages 101–104 before moving on to the section test on page 108.
	0–4 answers correct	**Oops!** Time to review what you have learned and try again. Review the practice section on pages 101–104. Then, retake the test on page 105. Now, move on to the section test on page 108.

Final Social Studies Test
for pages 81–104

DIRECTIONS: Choose the best answer.

1. **Which of the following is not a stereotype?**

   (A) Gang violence is a serious problem in many poor communities.

   (B) Muslims hate America.

   (C) Librarians are quiet and fussy.

   (D) People who live in the country are friendlier than people who live in big cities.

2. **Which of the following groups and institutions has the least amount of influence on current American society?**

   (F) universities

   (G) labor unions

   (H) churches

   (J) temperance groups

3. **In the United States, the median age for a woman marrying for the first time is _____ .**

   (A) 18

   (B) 26

   (C) 35

   (D) 40

4. **The Organization of American States has _____ member nations.**

   (F) 25

   (G) 30

   (H) 35

   (J) 40

5. **What is the name of the political and economic alliance formed by European nations?**

   (A) Alliance of European States

   (B) European Alliance

   (C) European Union

   (D) European Treaty Organization

6. **An entrepreneur is someone who _____ .**

   (F) starts a business

   (G) runs a business

   (H) assumes the risk for a business

   (J) all of the above

DIRECTIONS: Study the chronology below and then answer questions 7–8.

Transportation in the United States	
1794	The first successful turnpike (toll road) opens.
1807	Robert Fulton's steam-powered boat, the *Clermont,* makes a round trip between Albany and New York in five days.
1825	The Erie Canal is completed.
1840	The United States has developed more than 3,000 miles of canals and 3,000 miles of railroad tracks.
1860	More than 30,000 miles of railroad track connect towns across the United States.
1892	Automobiles powered by gasoline are invented.

7. **Which happened first?**

   (A) Automobiles chugged across the country.

   (B) The Erie Canal was completed.

   (C) The *Clermont* sailed.

   (D) The United States laid more than 30,000 miles of railroad tracks.

8. **How many years passed between the time the United States developed 3,000 miles of railroad tracks and 30,000 miles of railroad tracks?**

   (F) 10 years

   (G) 15 years

   (H) 20 years

   (J) 50 years

DIRECTIONS: Choose the best answer.

9. **As a citizen, you have a responsibility to take part in your community. All of the following are good ways to do this except _____ .**

   (A) write a letter to the editor of your local newspaper

   (B) read the newspaper regularly

   (C) secretly remove books from the library that you think are unpatriotic

   (D) vote in every election

10. **Which of the following groups has had the least amount of influence on the music, art, food, religion, and language of the United States?**

    (F) Australians

    (G) Africans

    (H) Native Americans

    (J) Europeans

11. **Which of the following political systems is based on the idea that the people rule?**

    (A) dictatorship

    (B) democracy

    (C) monarchy

    (D) theocracy

12. **"Separation of powers" means that _____ .**

    (F) power is divided between national and state governments

    (G) power is divided among the legislative, executive, and judicial branches of government

    (H) executive power is divided between the president, vice-president, and members of the cabinet

    (J) legislative power is divided between the Senate and House of Representatives

13. **Which amendment to the U.S. Constitution protects citizens against self-incrimination?**

    (A) First Amendment

    (B) Second Amendment

    (C) Fifth Amendment

    (D) Eighth Amendment

DIRECTIONS: Read the news story below. Then, answer questions 14–15.

The most popular snack food in years has recently hit the stores. Everyone wants to try the new Beef-o Chips. These hamburger-flavored potato chips are so popular, the manufacturer is having a hard time keeping up with demand. Grocery stores across the nation have been mobbed by hungry customers looking to buy bags of Beef-os. The local Food Clown store reports that an entire shelf of Beef-os was bought out by customers yesterday in about five minutes.

14. **When Beef-os first came out a couple of months ago, each bag cost $1.99. Based on the information in the passage, what do you think Beef-os might be selling for now?**

    (F) 25¢

    (G) 99¢

    (H) $1.99

    (J) $2.99

15. **Explain your answer to question 14.**

    (A) Hamburger-flavored potato chips? Yuck! Who would buy those?

    (B) When supply is high and demand is low, prices usually go down.

    (C) The price was $1.99 just a couple of months ago. That's too soon for any price change to occur.

    (D) When supply is low and demand is high, prices usually rise.

GO

Name _____ Date _____

DIRECTIONS: Study the map below and then answer questions 16–19.

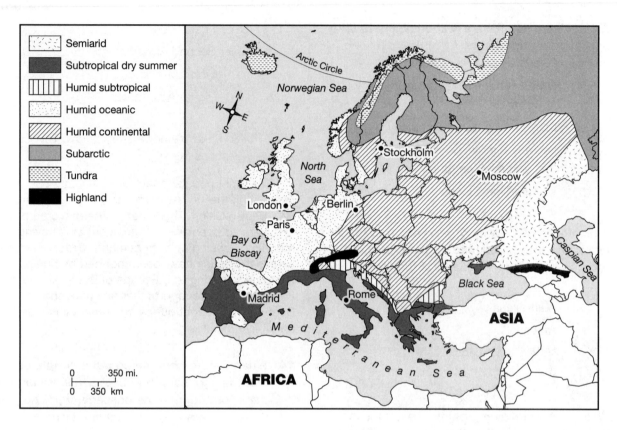

16. **A semiarid region is found near _____ .**

    Ⓕ Stockholm

    Ⓖ Paris

    Ⓗ Madrid

    Ⓙ Rome

17. **Dry summers are characteristic of the region bordering the _____ .**

    Ⓐ Bay of Biscay

    Ⓑ North Sea

    Ⓒ Baltic Sea

    Ⓓ Mediterranean Sea

18. **From the map, we can conclude that the climate of western Europe is mainly _____ .**

    Ⓕ humid

    Ⓖ dry

    Ⓗ hot

    Ⓙ unfit for human habitation

19. **The tundra lies close to the North Pole. It is an extremely cold, dry region, sometimes called a *cold desert*. The soil is not very fertile. Only the top portion of the soil thaws during the short, cold summer. Based on these facts, which of the following statements is most likely to be true?**

    Ⓐ Tall evergreen trees with deep roots thrive in the tundra.

    Ⓑ The tundra is too cold and dry to support any plant or animal life whatsoever.

    Ⓒ Tundra plants are adapted to drought and cold and tend to consist of mosses, grasses, and small shrubs.

    Ⓓ The tundra is the most biologically diverse place in the world.

STOP

Name _____ Date _____

Final Social Studies Test

Answer Sheet

1 (A) (B) (C) (D)
2 (F) (G) (H) (J)
3 (A) (B) (C) (D)
4 (F) (G) (H) (J)
5 (A) (B) (C) (D)
6 (F) (G) (H) (J)
7 (A) (B) (C) (D)
8 (F) (G) (H) (J)
9 (A) (B) (C) (D)
10 (F) (G) (H) (J)

11 (A) (B) (C) (D)
12 (F) (G) (H) (J)
13 (A) (B) (C) (D)
14 (F) (G) (H) (J)
15 (A) (B) (C) (D)
16 (F) (G) (H) (J)
17 (A) (B) (C) (D)
18 (F) (G) (H) (J)
19 (A) (B) (C) (D)

Science Standards

Standard 1—Unifying Concepts and Processes *(See pages 114–115.)*
As a result of the activities in grades K–12, all students should develop understanding and abilities aligned with the following concepts and processes:
- Systems, order, and organization.
- Evidence, models, and explanation.
- Constancy, change, and measurement.
- Evolution and equilibrium.
- Form and function.

Standard 2—Science as Inquiry *(See pages 116–117.)*
As a result of their activities in grades 5–8, all students should develop
- Abilities necessary to do scientific inquiry.
- Understandings about scientific inquiry.

Standard 3—Physical Science *(See pages 119–121.)*
As a result of their activities in grades 5–8, all students should develop an understanding of
- Properties and changes of properties in matter.
- Motion and forces.
- Transfer of energy.

Standard 4—Life Science *(See pages 122–123.)*
As a result of their activities in grades 5–8, all students should develop an understanding of
- Structure and function in living systems.
- Reproduction and heredity.
- Regulation and behavior.
- Populations and ecosystems.
- Diversity and adaptations of organisms.

Standard 5—Earth and Space Science *(See pages 124–126.)*
As a result of their activities in grades 5–8, all students should develop an understanding of
- Structure of the Earth system.
- Earth's history.
- Earth in the solar system.

Standard 6—Science and Technology *(See page 128.)*
As a result of their activities in grades 5–8, all students should develop
- Abilities of technological design.
- Understandings about science and technology.

Standard 7—Science in Personal and Social Perspectives *(See page 129.)*
As a result of their activities in grades 5–8, all students should develop an understanding of
- Personal health.
- Populations, resources, and environments.
- Natural hazards.
- Risks and benefits.
- Science and technology in society.

Science Standards

Standard 8—History and Nature of Science *(See page 130.)*
As a result of their activities in grades 5–8, all students should develop an understanding of

- Science as a human endeavor.
- Nature of science.
- History of science.

Science

1.0

Constancy and Change

Unifying Concepts and Processes

DIRECTIONS: Choose the best answer.

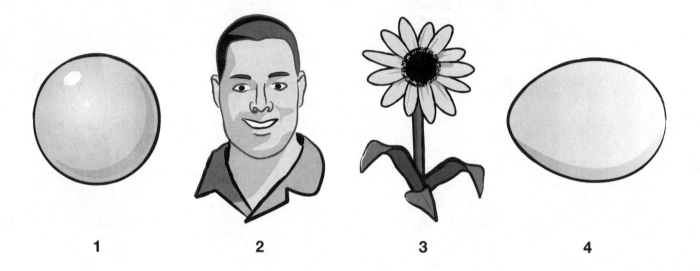

1   2   3   4

1. **Which of the items shown above has the greatest constancy of form?**

   (A)   item 1

   (B)   item 2

   (C)   item 3

   (D)   item 4

2. **In an explosion of a charge of dynamite, what remains constant?**

   (F)   the total mass of all the products

   (G)   the momentum of all the products

   (H)   the energy of all the products

   (J)   all of the above

3. **Scientists refer to a sequence of changes that happens over and over as _____ .**

   (A)   symmetry

   (B)   a trend

   (C)   a cycle

   (D)   chaos

4. **Which of the following is an example of steady change?**

   (F)   the number of molecules in the universe

   (G)   the speed of a falling rock

   (H)   the vibration of a guitar string

   (J)   the speed of light

STOP

Science

| 1.0 |

Identifying Simple Systems
Unifying Concepts and Processes

DIRECTIONS: Anything with parts that interact is called a *system*. In the list below, write **S** in the blank if it is a system. Write **N** if it is not a system.

_____ 1. yo-yo

_____ 2. pencil

_____ 3. rock

_____ 4. motorcycle engine

_____ 5. dog's eye

_____ 6. alphabet

_____ 7. pond

_____ 8. rubber ball

_____ 9. rollerskate

_____ 10. drawing

_____ 11. tree

_____ 12. calculator

_____ 13. wheelbarrow

_____ 14. elephant's ear

_____ 15. desk

_____ 16. language

_____ 17. school

DIRECTIONS: Answer the following question.

18. Describe the parts of a skateboard and how they interact to make it a system.

_____

_____

_____

_____

_____

_____

_____

_____

_____

_____

_____

_____

_____

_____

_____

_____

_____

_____

_____

_____

_____

_____

_____

_____

STOP

Name _____   Date _____

The Process of Scientific Inquiry

Science as Inquiry

DIRECTIONS: Choose the best answer.

1. Jordan lives in a desert and wants to find out if the area has always been a desert. He spends one afternoon gathering rocks and brings them home to study. This is an example of which kind of scientific investigation?

   (A)   observation

   (B)   experimentation

   (C)   collecting specimens for analysis

   (D)   none of these

2. Jeannie wanted to find out if warm water was more dense than cold water. She added red food coloring to a beaker of warm water and then used an eyedropper to add the warm, red water to a beaker of cold water. This is an example of what kind of scientific investigation?

   (F)   observation

   (G)   experimentation

   (H)   collecting specimens for analysis

   (J)   none of these

3. You are boiling water on your stove next to a window. You notice water droplets on the inside of the window. This is an example of what kind of scientific investigation?

   (A)   observation

   (B)   experimentation

   (C)   collecting specimens for analysis

   (D)   none of these

4. Susan wants to learn more about molecules. She reads an article about molecules in the encyclopedia. This is an example of what kind of scientific investigation?

   (F)   observation

   (G)   experimentation

   (H)   collecting specimens for analysis

   (J)   none of these

5. Which of the following instruments would be used to study cells?

   (A)   telescope

   (B)   microscope

   (C)   binoculars

   (D)   thermometer

6. Which of the following instruments would be used to examine the features of the Moon?

   (F)   binoculars

   (G)   microscope

   (H)   thermometer

   (J)   telescope

7. It is important for scientists to keep accurate and detailed records so _____ .

   (A)   they can decide which scientists they want to work with on future projects

   (B)   they can decide who the best scientist is

   (C)   more scientists can have jobs

   (D)   the results of the experiments can be verified

Name _____ Date _____

Science

Similar Scientific Investigations

Science as Inquiry

DIRECTIONS: Read the story below, and then answer the questions that follow.

> Lauren entered the science fair. For her project, she wanted to see which brand of batteries lasts longest: Everglo, Glomore, or Everlasting. She decided to place new batteries into identical new flashlights, turn on the flashlights, then wait for the batteries to run down. She wrote down the following results: Everglo—lasted 19 hours; Glomore—lasted 17 hours; Everlasting—lasted 25 hours.
>
> She then decided to redo the experiment to confirm the results. For her second experiment, she placed new batteries into the old flashlights that her parents keep in the garage, the kitchen, and their bedroom. She then turned on the flashlights and waited for the batteries to run down. This time she wrote down the following results: Everglo—lasted 13 hours; Glomore—lasted 16 hours; Everlasting—lasted 9 hours.
>
> Lauren was puzzled by the results of her second experiment. Because it was so similar to her first experiment, she thought she would get the same results.

1. **What is the best explanation for why Lauren's second experiment had different results than her first experiment?**

   (A) Lauren used different brands of batteries in the second experiment.

   (B) The second experiment used old flashlights, while the first experiment used new flashlights.

   (C) The second experiment was too much like the first experiment.

   (D) There is no good explanation; sometimes things just happen.

2. **How was Lauren sure that the results of the second experiment were different from the results of the first experiment?**

   (F) She read on the side of the battery packages how long each brand would last before it ran down.

   (G) She simply remembered how long it took each brand of battery to run down.

   (H) She recorded exactly how long it took each brand of battery to run down for each experiment.

   (J) She cannot be sure; her experiment was faulty.

3. **Tell what Lauren did right in her experiments.**

   _____

   _____

   _____

   _____

   _____

   _____

4. **Could she have done anything in a better, more scientific way?**

   _____

   _____

   _____

   _____

Science

| 1.0–2.0 |

For pages 114–117

Mini-Test 1

Unifying Concepts and Processes; Science as Inquiry

DIRECTIONS: Choose the best answer.

1. **Which of the following is the best definition of a *system*?**
   - (A) the total characteristics of an organism
   - (B) a recurring sequence of events
   - (C) a collection of interacting parts
   - (D) a theoretical description of a complex process

2. **Which of the following is not a system?**
   - (F) rubber band
   - (G) book
   - (H) MP3 player
   - (J) your leg

3. **Which of the following is a type of constancy?**
   - (A) symmetry
   - (B) growth
   - (C) a cycle
   - (D) chaos

4. **Adam wants to find out how lemon juice reacts when it is combined with different substances. In three separate paper cups, he puts equal amounts of baking soda, salt, and sugar. Then, he puts 3 drops of lemon juice into each cup. This is an example of what kind of scientific investigation?**
   - (F) observation
   - (G) experimentation
   - (H) collecting specimens for analysis
   - (J) none of the above

5. **What instrument do scientists use to study single-celled organisms?**
   - (A) telescope
   - (B) microscope
   - (C) binoculars
   - (D) thermometer

DIRECTIONS: Read the passage below to answer questions 6 and 7.

Ryan wants to find out if people can tell the difference between the taste of cold tap water and cold bottled water. He fills one glass pitcher with tap water and another glass pitcher with bottled water. Then, he places the pitchers in the same refrigerator overnight.

6. **What should be the next step in Ryan's experiment?**
   - (F) He should ask several people to taste the tap water.
   - (G) He should ask several people to taste the bottled water.
   - (H) He should ask several people to taste both types of water and guess which one is tap water and which one is bottled water.
   - (J) He should ask several people to taste both types of water and tell which one they like the best.

7. **If Ryan repeats his experiment, will he get exactly the same results? Explain your answer.**

   _____

   _____

   _____

   _____

   _____

STOP

Science

3.0

Force and Newton's Laws of Motion

Physical Science

DIRECTIONS: Read the passage below, and then answer the questions that follow.

Isaac Newton (1643–1727) was an English physicist, mathematician, and philosopher. He is regarded by most as one of the most influential scientists in history. His famous three laws of motion are the basis of the study of physics.

- Newton's First Law states that an object at rest tends to stay at rest and that an object that is in motion tends to stay in motion unless acted upon by an unbalanced force.
- Newton's Second Law states that F=ma, or force equals mass times acceleration. In other words, the rate of change of momentum is proportional to the imposed force and goes in the direction of the force.
- Newton's Third Law states that whenever one body exerts a force on another, the second body exerts the same amount of force in the opposite direction.

1. **You are a passenger in a car. The driver suddenly slams on the brakes. You keep moving forward until your seat belt stops you from going through the windshield. Which of Newton's laws does this demonstrate?**

    (A) First Law

    (B) Second Law

    (C) Third Law

    (D) none of the above

2. **Three pro football players pushing a stalled truck can get it going faster than if only one were pushing. Which of Newton's laws does this demonstrate?**

    (F) First Law

    (G) Second Law

    (H) Third Law

    (J) none of the above

3. **The push or pull that is needed to start or stop something moving is called _____ .**

    (A) force

    (B) energy

    (C) inertia

    (D) motion

4. **The tendency of an object to remain moving in a straight line at constant speed or to remain stationary is called _____ .**

    (F) gravity

    (G) friction

    (H) inertia

    (J) acceleration

5. **A kind of force that slows things down is called _____ .**

    (A) mass

    (B) friction

    (C) acceleration

    (D) inertia

STOP

Science

3.0

Transfer of Energy
Physical Science

DIRECTIONS: Choose the best answer.

1. **One definition of *energy* is _____ .**

   (A) the ability to make things happen

   (B) any substance that takes up space

   (C) a force that cannot be transferred to another object

   (D) any substance that cannot be changed into a different substance

2. **A toaster changes _____ energy into _____ energy.**

   (F) chemical, potential

   (G) kinetic, electrical

   (H) electrical, heat and light

   (J) chemical, electrical

3. **If you stir a hot pan of soup with a cold spoon, the spoon will become warm because of _____ .**

   (A) conduction

   (B) chemical energy

   (C) insulation

   (D) convection

4. **The sun transfers energy through space by _____ .**

   (F) photosynthesis

   (G) conduction

   (H) convection

   (J) radiation

5. **The moment a boulder starts to fall from the top of a cliff, the potential energy in the boulder _____ and the kinetic energy _____ .**

   (A) stays the same, increases

   (B) decreases, stays the same

   (C) decreases, increases

   (D) increases, decreases

6. **The wind that is formed when cold air sinks and warm air rises is an example of _____ .**

   (F) potential energy

   (G) convection

   (H) conduction

   (J) radiation

Figure 1   **Figure 2**   **Figure 3**

7. **Which of the above figures shows the ball with the most potential energy?**

   (A) Figure 1

   (B) Figure 2

   (C) Figure 3

   (D) All the balls have the same amount of potential energy.

STOP

Science

3.0

Types of Matter
Physical Science

DIRECTIONS: The table below gives definitions for the various types of matter. Use the table to answer the questions that follow.

Matter			
Anything with mass and volume			
Element	**Compound**	**Mixture**	**Solution**
A substance made up of only one type of atom	Two or more elements that are chemically combined	Two or more substances that are physically combined; they are heterogeneous (have areas of differing compositions)	Two or more substances that are physically combined; they are homogeneous (have a constant composition)

DIRECTIONS: Classify each of the substances below as an element, compound, mixture, or solution.

1. pizza _____

2. salt _____

3. sodium bicarbonate _____

4. vegetable soup _____

5. soda pop _____

6. carbon monoxide _____

7. carbon _____

8. oxygen _____

9. soil _____

10. salt water _____

11. **In a glass of salt water, which of the following is the solvent?**

   Ⓐ salt

   Ⓑ water

   Ⓒ heat

   Ⓓ glass

12. **In a glass of salt water, which of the following is the solute?**

   Ⓕ salt

   Ⓖ water

   Ⓗ heat

   Ⓙ glass

13. **Explain why pure water is a compound and not a mixture or solution.**

   _____

   _____

   _____

   _____

   _____

STOP

Science

4.0

The Web of Life
Life Science

DIRECTIONS: Choose the best answer.

Clue

Photosynthesis can be expressed by the chemical equation below:

carbon dioxide + water + light energy → glucose (sugar) + oxygen + water

Photosynthesis	
Energy Source	Sunlight
Raw Materials	
Products	

1. **In the table above, which of the following correctly completes the "Raw Materials" row?**

   Ⓐ water

   Ⓑ carbon dioxide and water

   Ⓒ sugar and oxygen

   Ⓓ oxygen and carbon dioxide

2. **In the table above, which of the following correctly completes the "Products" row?**

   Ⓕ carbon dioxide and water

   Ⓖ water

   Ⓗ sugar, water, and oxygen

   Ⓙ oxygen and carbon dioxide

3. **What product of photosynthesis is released by the plant as waste?**

   Ⓐ oxygen

   Ⓑ sugar

   Ⓒ carbon dioxide

   Ⓓ water

4. **Excess sugar produced by photosynthesis _____ .**

   Ⓕ is released by the plant as a waste product

   Ⓖ is converted back into carbon dioxide and water

   Ⓗ is stored in plants as other sugars and starches

   Ⓙ weakens the plant's structure and slowly causes it to die

5. **Why cannot a plant's root cells usually make food for the plant?**

   Ⓐ They are not alive.

   Ⓑ They normally lack chlorophyll.

   Ⓒ They have too many chloroplasts.

   Ⓓ All of the above are true.

6. **Organisms that are capable of photosynthesis _____ .**

   Ⓕ are always the last step in a food chain

   Ⓖ cannot make their own food

   Ⓗ are the first organisms eaten in a food chain

   Ⓙ are not part of any food chains or food webs

GO

Name _____ Date _____

DIRECTIONS: Use the food web below to answer questions 7–10.

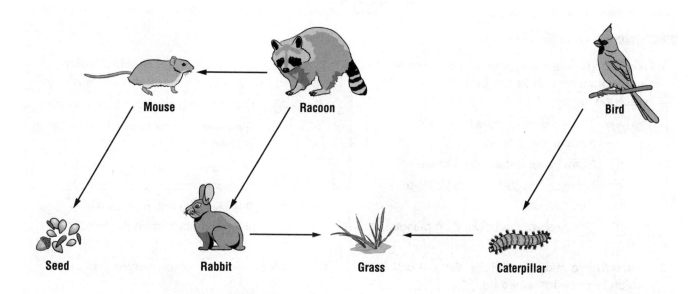

7. **In the food web above, how do the grasses obtain their food?**

   Ⓐ through chemosynthesis

   Ⓑ by eating the caterpillars

   Ⓒ by consuming wastes and dead organisms in the soil

   Ⓓ through photosynthesis

8. **Which organisms in the food web obtain their energy, either directly or indirectly, from the grasses?**

   Ⓕ caterpillars, rabbits, raccoons, birds

   Ⓖ mice

   Ⓗ caterpillars and rabbits

   Ⓙ birds

9. **When a rabbit in the food web eats grasses, what happens to most of the energy in the grasses?**

   Ⓐ It is transferred to the raccoon when the raccoon eats the rabbit.

   Ⓑ The rabbit uses it for its own life processes.

   Ⓒ It is excreted by the rabbit as waste.

   Ⓓ It is recycled by the rabbit.

10. **In the food web above, which two organisms are potential competitors for food?**

    Ⓕ the caterpillar and the rabbit

    Ⓖ the rabbit and the mouse

    Ⓗ the bird and the raccoon

    Ⓙ the grasses and the caterpillar

Science

5.0

Earth and the Solar System
Earth and Space Science

DIRECTIONS: Choose the best answer.

1. **Why do stars appear as small points of light in the night sky, while the planets appear to be much larger?**

   (A) There are more stars in our solar system than planets.

   (B) Stars travel faster than planets.

   (C) Stars are much farther from Earth than planets.

   (D) Stars reflect more light than planets.

2. **The sun is a star in the Milky Way galaxy, which is best described as _____ .**

   (F) a dwarf galaxy

   (G) a spiral galaxy

   (H) an elliptical galaxy

   (J) a massive galaxy

3. **The large craters on the surface of the Moon and the planet Mercury are most likely caused by _____ .**

   (A) giant lava flows

   (B) asteroid impacts

   (C) nuclear explosions

   (D) large collapsed caves

4. **Why is the Moon very hot on the side facing the sun and very cold on the side facing away from the sun?**

   (F) The moon is made of thermal rocks.

   (G) The moon has a thin atmosphere.

   (H) The moon is made of reflective rocks.

   (J) The moon has no volcanic activity.

5. **Why do polar regions receive less solar energy than regions along the equator?**

   (A) The polar regions have less land area.

   (B) The polar regions have less vegetation to absorb sunlight.

   (C) The regions along the equator have days with more hours of sunlight.

   (D) The rays of the sun strike the regions along the equator vertically.

6. **Which of these revolves around a planet?**

   (F) an asteroid

   (G) a star

   (H) a comet

   (J) a moon

7. **In making a model of our solar system, a tennis ball could represent Earth and a marble could represent Mercury because _____ .**

   (A) compared to Earth, Mercury is much smaller

   (B) compared to Earth, Mercury is much harder

   (C) compared to Mercury, Earth is much greener

   (D) compared to Mercury, Earth is much denser

GO

Name _____ Date _____

DIRECTIONS: Study the diagrams below and answer the questions.

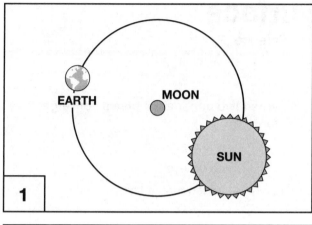

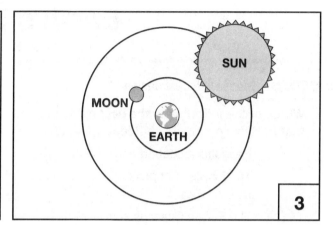

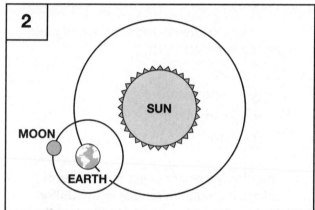

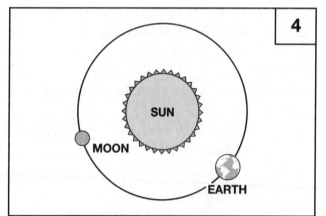

8. **Which diagram shows the relationship between the sun, the Moon, and Earth?**

(F) 1

(G) 2

(H) 3

(J) 4

9. **The arrows in the diagram above show the movement of the wind from the poles. What causes the wind to deflect from the North and South Poles?**

(A) the rotation of Earth on its axis

(B) the shape of Earth

(C) the tilt of Earth's axis

(D) the difference in landmass in each hemisphere

STOP

Name _____   Date _____

Science
5.0

Investigating Earth's Surface
Earth and Space Science

DIRECTIONS: Choose the best answer.

1. **Which of the following is the best evidence that Earth's continents shifted long ago?**

   (A) Penguins are found only in Antarctica.

   (B) The fossils of tropical plants are found in Antarctica.

   (C) The Pacific Ocean is surrounded by volcanoes.

   (D) Rivers form deltas because of continental erosion.

2. **Why are most fossils found in sedimentary rocks?**

   (F) Sedimentary rocks are Earth's most common rocks.

   (G) Organisms normally live in areas with sedimentary rock.

   (H) Organisms can be trapped and preserved in sedimentary rock.

   (J) Sedimentary rocks are found closest to the surface of Earth.

3. **Earthquake vibrations are detected, measured, and recorded by instruments called _____ .**

   (A) sonargraphs

   (B) seismographs

   (C) Richter scales

   (D) magnetometers

4. **When two continental plates converge, they form _____ .**

   (F) island arcs

   (G) rift valleys

   (H) folded mountains

   (J) trenches

5. **A mixture of weathered rock and organic matter is called _____ .**

   (A) soil

   (B) limestone

   (C) carbon dioxide

   (D) clay

6. **Christopher was looking at pictures of different mountain ranges in the United States. He was surprised to see that the Appalachian Mountains were smaller and more rounded than the Rocky Mountains. The Appalachian Mountains looked old and worn compared to the Rocky Mountains. What is the best explanation?**

   (F) The effects of the wind and water caused weathering, wearing away the mountains.

   (G) Too many people and animals traveled across the mountains, causing them to wear away.

   (H) All of the snowfall was so heavy that it weighted down the mountains and caused them to shrink.

   (J) The water that used to cover Earth wore away parts of the mountains.

STOP

Science

| 3.0–5.0 |

For pages 119–126

Mini-Test 2

**Physical Science; Life Science;
Earth and Space Science**

DIRECTIONS: Choose the best answer.

1. **Which of the following statements about compounds is not true?**

   Ⓐ They consist of atoms of two or more different elements bound together.

   Ⓑ They cannot be broken down into simpler types of matter.

   Ⓒ They have properties that are different from their component elements.

   Ⓓ They always contain the same ratio of component atoms.

2. **Plants affect the life processes of nearly all the other organisms on Earth because they _____ .**

   Ⓕ provide either direct or indirect food sources for most other organisms

   Ⓖ remove large amounts of oxygen from the atmosphere

   Ⓗ release large amounts of carbon dioxide into the atmosphere

   Ⓙ all of the above are true

3. **Heat energy is transferred by _____ .**

   Ⓐ convection

   Ⓑ conduction

   Ⓒ radiation

   Ⓓ all of the above

4. **Inertia is _____ .**

   Ⓕ the push or pull that is needed to start or stop something moving

   Ⓖ the tendency of an object to remain moving in a straight line at constant speed or to remain stationary

   Ⓗ a kind of force that slows things down

   Ⓙ the attractive force of an object

5. **What would happen if Earth's axis were not tilted, but straight up and down?**

   Ⓐ Nothing would change.

   Ⓑ Earth would not have seasons.

   Ⓒ It would always be summer on Earth.

   Ⓓ It would always be winter on Earth.

6. **Look at the picture below. It shows high mountains. The layers are made of sedimentary rock. Before the mountains were formed, the sedimentary rocks were in flat layers. How were the mountains formed?**

   Ⓕ The rock layers were pushed down.

   Ⓖ The rock layers were pulled apart.

   Ⓗ The rock layers were pushed up.

   Ⓙ The rock layers went in opposite directions.

STOP

Science

6.0

Consequences of Technology

Science and Technology

DIRECTIONS: Many different people in different cultures have been involved in science and technology. To learn more about their contributions, use the library or Internet to complete the tables below.

1. **Transportation**—Research three inventions related to transportation.

Invention	Date	Inventor	Nationality

2. **Communication**—Research three inventions used for communication.

Invention	Date	Inventor	Nationality

3. **Health/Medicine**—Research three inventions or developments related to medicine.

Invention	Date	Inventor	Nationality

4. **Entertainment**—Research three inventions that are used for entertainment.

Invention	Date	Inventor	Nationality

5. **Now pick one of the inventions you found and write a one-page paper describing some of its intended and unintended consequences.**

STOP

Name _____ Date _____

Science

7.0

Using and Conserving Resources

Science in Personal and Social Perspectives

DIRECTIONS: Choose the best answer.

 Clue   **Nonrenewable resources** are ones that cannot be quickly replaced by natural processes. **Renewable resources** are ones that are recycled or replaced by natural processes.

1. **What natural resources are saved by recycling paper?**
   - (A) water and trees
   - (B) landfill space
   - (C) the oil used by power machinery
   - (D) all of the above

2. **Fossil fuels are examples of _____ .**
   - (F) renewable resources
   - (G) nonrenewable resources
   - (H) inexhaustible resources
   - (J) none of these

3. **Alternative sources of energy include all of the following except _____ .**
   - (A) wind
   - (B) water
   - (C) sun
   - (D) soil

4. **Water, wind, and solar energy are all examples of _____ .**
   - (F) renewable resources
   - (G) nonrenewable resources
   - (H) inexhaustible resources
   - (J) none of the above

DIRECTIONS: Match each of the activities below with the amount of water it consumes.

____ 5. **Flush the toilet.**

____ 6. **Brush your teeth.**

____ 7. **Use the dishwasher.**

____ 8. **Take a shower or bath.**

____ 9. **Wash the car.**

A. 17–24 gallons
B. 1.5–4 gallons
C. 50 gallons
D. 8–15 gallons
E. 2–5 gallons

10. **Use the chart below to keep a record of the water you use for one day.**

Activity (brushing teeth, getting a drink, etc.)	Amount of Water Used

11. **After compiling the chart, list at least two ways you could save water each day.**

_____

_____

STOP

Science

8.0

The Formulation
of Cell Theory

History and Nature of Science

DIRECTIONS: Study the table below about important events in the formulation of cell theory and then answer the questions that follow.

Date	Event
Late 1500s	First microscope invented
1665	Robert Hooke observed cork under a microscope; cork appeared to be made up of little boxes, which he called *cells.*
1680s	Antonie van Leeuwenhoek saw living organisms in pond water through his simple microscope.
1830s	After studying plant parts through his microscope, Matthias Schleiden concluded that all plants are made of cells.
1830s	After observing animal cells through his microscope, Theodore Schwann concluded that all animals are made of cells.
1850s	Rudolf Virchow hypothesized that cells divide to form new cells.

1. **The table indicates that Rudolf Virchow's major contribution to cell theory was**

   _____ .

   (A) the invention of the microscope

   (B) the hypothesis that all living things are made of cells

   (C) the coining of the word *cell*

   (D) the idea that all cells come from preexisting cells

2. **Based on the table, we can conclude that**

   _____ .

   (F) the microscope was not important in the study of cells

   (G) the main components of cell theory had been established by the middle of the 19th century

   (H) the notion that all living things are made of cells was developed in the late 1600s

   (J) Leeuwenhoek proved that all plants are made of cells

3. **Based on the table, who first concluded that all plants are made of cells?**

   (A) Rudolf Virchow

   (B) Matthias Schleiden

   (C) Antonie van Leeuwenhoek

   (D) Theodor Schwann

4. **Cell theory would not have developed without the invention of the _____ .**

   (F) kaleidoscope

   (G) stethoscope

   (H) microscope

   (J) telescope

5. **With whose observations did Theodor Schwann combine his own ideas to conclude that all living things are made of cells?**

   (A) Robert Hooke

   (B) Antonie van Leeuwenhoek

   (C) Rudolf Virchow

   (D) Matthias Schleiden

STOP

Science

6.0–8.0

For pages 128–130

Mini-Test 3

**Science and Technology; Science in Personal
and Social Perspectives; History and Nature of Science**

DIRECTIONS: Read the passage below to answer question 1.

Instead of trying to control pests with chemicals, some farmers introduce organisms from other ecosystems in an effort to reduce the number of pests in the agricultural ecosystem. One example of this is the use of foreign insects that feed on local weeds. This approach also carries some risk, because an introduced organism may become a pest itself.

1. **What can you conclude from the passage?**
   - (A) Technology causes more problems than it solves.
   - (B) Technological innovations generally carry some risks.
   - (C) Scientists always know how technological innovations are going to turn out.
   - (D) The link between science and technology is slight.

DIRECTIONS: Choose the best answer.

2. **Which of the following is a renewable energy source?**
   - (F) natural gas
   - (G) oil
   - (H) coal
   - (J) wind

3. **Which of the following helps conserve natural resources?**
   - (A) using less water
   - (B) developing alternative energy sources
   - (C) recycling
   - (D) all of the above

4. **Robert Hooke's major contribution to cell theory was _____ .**
   - (F) the hypothesis that all living things are made of cells
   - (G) the invention of the microscope
   - (H) the coining of the word *cell*
   - (J) the discovery of DNA

5. **Which of the following events occurred first?**
   - (A) Theodore Schwann concluded that all animals are made of cells.
   - (B) Rudolf Virchow hypothesized that cells divide to form new cells.
   - (C) Matthias Schleiden concluded that all plants are made of cells.
   - (D) The first microscope was invented.

6. **For each of the following areas, list one invention, its inventor, and the inventor's nationality:**

   Transportation

   _____

   _____

   Communication

   _____

   _____

   Health/Medicine

   _____

   _____

   Entertainment

   _____

   _____

   STOP

How Am I Doing?

Mini-Test 1 Page 118 **Number Correct**	7 answers correct	**Great Job!** Move on to the section test on page 133.
	5–6 answers correct	**You're almost there!** But you still need a little practice. Review practice pages 114–117 before moving on to the section test on page 133.
	0–4 answers correct	**Oops!** Time to review what you have learned and try again. Review the practice section on pages 114–117. Then, retake the test on page 118. Now, move on to the section test on page 133.
Mini-Test 2 Page 127 **Number Correct**	7 answers correct	**Awesome!** Move on to the section test on page 133.
	5–6 answers correct	**You're almost there!** But you still need a little practice. Review practice pages 119–126 before moving on to the section test on page 133.
	0–4 answers correct	**Oops!** Time to review what you have learned and try again. Review the practice section on pages 119–126. Then, retake the test on page 127. Now, move on to the section test on page 133.
Mini-Test 3 Page 131 **Number Correct**	6 answers correct	**Great Job!** Move on to the section test on page 133.
	4–5 answers correct	**You're almost there!** But you still need a little practice. Review practice pages 128–130 before moving on to the section test on page 133.
	0–3 answers correct	**Oops!** Time to review what you have learned and try again. Review the practice section on pages 128–130. Then, retake the test on page 131. Now, move on to the section test on page 133.

Name _____   Date _____

Final Science Test
for pages 114–130

DIRECTIONS: Read the passage below and then answer questions 1–4.

Earth is a restless place. Although it may seem perfectly solid to you, the ground below your feet is moving at this very moment! The continents rest on top of the brittle crust of Earth, which has broken apart into pieces. These pieces, called *tectonic plates,* float around on top of the molten interior of the earth, much like crackers floating in a bowl of soup. Molten rock continues to push up through cracks in the plates, pushing the plates even farther apart. Over 200 million years ago, the continents were connected together as one piece of land. Over the years, they have split off and drifted farther and farther apart, at the rate of about one inch every year.

1. **According to this passage, why do tectonic plates move around?**
   - (A) They are floating on water.
   - (B) Molten rock pushes up through the cracks and pushes them apart.
   - (C) The continents are trying to connect together again.
   - (D) The crust of Earth is breaking.

2. **What piece of evidence would help scientists prove that the continents used to be connected?**
   - (F) finding similar fossils on the coasts of two different continents
   - (G) having a photograph of the two continents connected
   - (H) measuring the temperature of the oceans
   - (J) timing how long it takes for a continent to move one inch

3. **What happened to Earth when its continents shifted?**
   - (A) Its climate regions changed.
   - (B) Its mass changed.
   - (C) The speed at which it orbits changed.
   - (D) Its position in the solar system changed.

4. **According to this passage, about how long would it take for Europe and North America to move one foot farther apart?**
   - (F) 6 years
   - (G) 8 years
   - (H) 10 years
   - (J) 12 years

DIRECTIONS: Choose the best answer.

5. **Which planet is smaller than Earth?**
   - (A) Saturn
   - (B) Neptune
   - (C) Mercury
   - (D) Jupiter

6. **Which of the following is a system?**
   - (F) a clock
   - (G) a spoon
   - (H) a ping-pong ball
   - (J) a piece of gum

7. **Matthias Schleiden, Theodore Schwann, and Rudolf Virchow all made major contributions in the field of _____ .**
   - (A) communication
   - (B) transportation
   - (C) cell theory
   - (D) astronomy

GO

Name _____ Date _____

DIRECTIONS: Read Jeannie's notes to answer questions 8–10.

Jeannie's Notes

My Question: Is warm water denser than cold water?
What I Already Know: If two objects take up the same amount of space, the lighter one will be less dense.
What I Did: I filled a beaker with 100 mL of cold water. Then, I filled another beaker with 100 mL of hot water, and I used red food coloring to color it red. I used an eyedropper to put the warm, red water into the beaker of cold water.
What Happened: The drops of red water floated to the top of the beaker. The red water made a layer on top of the layer of cold water in the beaker.

8. **This is an example of what kind of scientific investigation?**
    (F) observation
    (G) experimentation
    (H) collection of specimens for analysis
    (J) none of the above

9. **From her notes, Jeannie can conclude that _____ .**
    (A) warm water is denser than cold water
    (B) warm water is less dense than cold water
    (C) warm water and cold water have the same density
    (D) neither warm nor cold water have any density

10. **What phenomena does this investigation help Jeannie understand?**
    (F) why it rains in the summer
    (G) why cold water boils so slowly
    (H) why the top layer of the ocean is warmer than the lower layers
    (J) why it is hard to make sugar dissolve in iced tea

DIRECTIONS: Choose the best answer.

11. **Sand is an example of a(n) _____ .**
    (A) compound
    (B) element
    (C) solution
    (D) mixture

12. **Mixtures and solutions must consist of at least _____ .**
    (F) one substance
    (G) two substances
    (H) three different elements
    (J) three different compounds

13. **All of the following are examples of constancy except _____ .**
    (A) the speed of light
    (B) the distance of the moon to Earth
    (C) the charge of an electron
    (D) the total mass plus energy in the universe

14. **When you recycle paper, you help keep the carbon dioxide-oxygen cycle running. Why is this statement true?**
    (F) When paper is recycled, the process releases oxygen back into the environment.
    (G) Carbon dioxide is trapped in the paper, and recycling releases it.
    (H) The machinery used to recycle paper releases oxygen.
    (J) Recycling paper saves trees, which use carbon dioxide and release oxygen.

15. **Energy that is possessed by an object due to its motion is called _____ .**
    (A) kinetic energy
    (B) potential energy
    (C) chemical energy
    (D) electrical energy

DIRECTIONS: Read the passage below to answer question 16.

The Law of Conservation of Mass and Energy, formulated in 1905 by Albert Einstein, states that whenever the amount of energy in one place decreases, the energy in another place increases by an equal amount.

16. **Based on the passage, you can conclude that which of the following statements is true?**

Ⓕ Energy cannot be changed into different forms.

Ⓖ There is more energy in deep space than in Earth's solar system.

Ⓗ Energy cannot be created or destroyed.

Ⓙ It is impossible to transfer energy from one object to another.

DIRECTIONS: Study the food web below to answer questions 17–18.

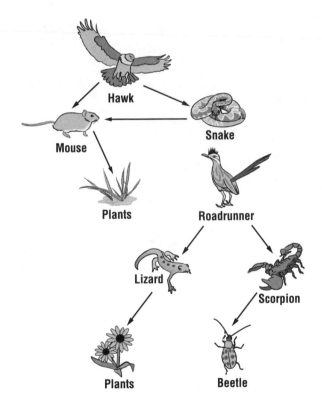

17. **The food web shows that the snake _____ .**

Ⓐ eats hawks

Ⓑ is food for the roadrunner

Ⓒ is food for the hawk

Ⓓ eats plants

18. **Which of the following events is most likely to occur if lizards are removed from the ecosystem illustrated in the food web?**

Ⓕ Roadrunners would eat more scorpions.

Ⓖ Scorpions would begin eating roadrunners.

Ⓗ Mice would stop eating plants.

Ⓙ All the animals in the ecosystem would die.

DIRECTIONS: Choose the best answer.

19. **A classmate argues that there is no relationship between photosynthesis and the life processes of carnivores. Which of the following would be a correct response?**

Ⓐ "Carnivores eat other animals, some of which obtain their energy directly from plants. So carnivores get their energy indirectly from plants."

Ⓑ "Carnivores make their own food through the process of photosynthesis."

Ⓒ "You're right; in fact, photosynthesis is unrelated to the life processes of all animals, not just carnivores."

Ⓓ "You're right, because carnivores do not eat any plants. Photosynthesis affects herbivores and omnivores only."

20. **Who developed the famous three laws of motion?**

Ⓕ Jonas Salk

Ⓖ Thomas Edison

Ⓗ Albert Einstein

Ⓙ Isaac Newton

STOP

Final Science Test

Answer Sheet

1 Ⓐ Ⓑ Ⓒ Ⓓ
2 Ⓕ Ⓖ Ⓗ Ⓙ
3 Ⓐ Ⓑ Ⓒ Ⓓ
4 Ⓕ Ⓖ Ⓗ Ⓙ
5 Ⓐ Ⓑ Ⓒ Ⓓ
6 Ⓕ Ⓖ Ⓗ Ⓙ
7 Ⓐ Ⓑ Ⓒ Ⓓ
8 Ⓕ Ⓖ Ⓗ Ⓙ
9 Ⓐ Ⓑ Ⓒ Ⓓ
10 Ⓕ Ⓖ Ⓗ Ⓙ

11 Ⓐ Ⓑ Ⓒ Ⓓ
12 Ⓕ Ⓖ Ⓗ Ⓙ
13 Ⓐ Ⓑ Ⓒ Ⓓ
14 Ⓕ Ⓖ Ⓗ Ⓙ
15 Ⓐ Ⓑ Ⓒ Ⓓ
16 Ⓕ Ⓖ Ⓗ Ⓙ
17 Ⓐ Ⓑ Ⓒ Ⓓ
18 Ⓕ Ⓖ Ⓗ Ⓙ
19 Ⓐ Ⓑ Ⓒ Ⓓ
20 Ⓕ Ⓖ Ⓗ Ⓙ

Answer Key

Pages 9–10
1. B
2. G
3. A
4. G
5. A
6. J
7. C
8. H
9. B
10. G

Pages 11–12
1. Rowan's pony is "little larger than a dog." She is referred to as a "child."
2. He is described as being "evil" and having a "huge form." When he speaks, the story says "he roared." One of the horsemen trembles in his presence.
3. Rowan calls the horsemen "raiders." The person who let her escape was punished. The lord says, "Be at ready with your blade."
4. H
5. A
6. J

Pages 13–14
Setting—Philadelphia
Main Characters—the brave little black-eyed rebel; the boy selling apples and potatoes
Plot—problem: She wanted to bring letters to the wives and children of the soldiers.

Plot—goal: The goal is to secretly pass the letters from the boy to the girl.
Episodes—(1) The boy came to the market. (2) The girl pretended to trade a kiss for a dozen apples. (3) The boy passed the letters to the girl.
Climax—The girl puts her arms around his neck in front of a watching crowd.
Resolution—He put the letters under her shawl, and she delivered them to waiting loved ones.

Page 15
1. B
2. H
3. D
4. H

Pages 16–17
1. D
2. G
3. C
4. F
5. Webs will vary.

Page 18 Mini-Test 1
1. B
2. F
3. C
4. H
5. B

Page 19
1. personal
2. indefinite
3. demonstrative
4. reflexive
5. possessive
6. personal
7. personal
8. interrogative
9. personal
10. demonstrative
11. interrogative
12. personal
13. possessive

Page 20
1. in the box
2. at city hall
3. under the bag
4. for the library book
5. to the applause; of the crowd
6.–9. Students' answers will vary but should include prepositional phrases appropriate for each sentence.
10. adjective
11. adjective
12. adverb
13. adjective
14. adverb
15. adjective
16. Students' paragraphs should provide detailed descriptions of their favorite places and should include a variety of adjectives and adverbs.

Page 21
1. was—LV
2. were—LV
3. lived—AV
4. grabbed, headed—AV
5. stopped—AV
6. was—LV, hit—AV
7. appears—LV, to be—LV
8. found—AV
9. became—LV
10. rode—AV
11. crashed—AV

For 12–21, the main verb is underlined. Helping verb is in boldfaced type.
12. **is** turning
13. **will be** coming
14. **is** getting
15. **might** look
16. **will** make
17. **should** go
18. **may** help
19. **had been** working
20. **could** drive
21. **should** be

Page 22
Students' compositions should provide at least three examples of the effects of the use of cellular phones on society. Each example should be supported with at least one detail or sample. Compositions should include logical order between sentences and have recognizable introductions, bodies, and conclusions.

Page 23
1. ran—dashed, darted, sprinted, bolted, rushed, flew, raced, charged
2. screamed—shouted, yelled, bellowed, roared, cheered
3. Answers will vary regarding how the word choice enhances the story. Possible answer: The different words present slightly different images; "running" is not the same as

"dashing" or "darting," for instance. The words also help clarify the character's personality; the reader gets a certain mental image of someone who "bellows" as opposed to someone who "hoarsely shouts."

Page 24
1. A
2. H
3. C
4. H

Pages 25–26
1. B
2. F
3. C
4. G
5. C
6. F
7. C
8. F
9. D
10. H
11. B
12. F
13. B
14. H
15. A
16. J
17. C
18. G
19. B
20. G

Pages 27–28
1. Mark Twain said, "Work consists of whatever a body is obliged to do. . . . Play consists of whatever a body is not obliged to do."
2. "April prepares her green traffic light, and the world thinks, *Go*," said Christopher Morley.
3. "That's one small step for a man,"

said Neil Armstrong, "and one giant leap for mankind."
4. "Injustice anywhere is a threat to justice everywhere," said Martin Luther King, Jr.
5. car, and
6. ahead; I
7. up, and
8. me; I
9. flying, but
10. At the grocery store, we need to buy the following: chicken, lettuce, and salad dressing.
11. Matthew likes pepperoni, onion, and green pepper on his pizza.
12. There are five people in our family: Mom, Dad, Jarad, Scott, and me.
13. B
14. J
15. C
16. G
17. C

Page 29 Mini-Test 2
1. A
2. F
3. D
4. G
5. B
6. F
7. B
8. H

Page 30
1. Answers will vary. Possible answers: Is the information presented as fact or opinion? Is any supporting evidence given for the claim? How old is the information?

2. Answers will vary, but most students should realize that the more recent articles will be more accurate and reliable than articles that are more than 80 years old.
3. Answers will vary. Most students will probably be skeptical of the story in the newspaper tabloid because such papers tend to present sensational stories that frequently are not well documented. They are not generally reliable sources of information.
4. If a story appeared in a respected paper such as *The New York Times,* most students would likely be more inclined to believe it.

Page 31
1. Answers will vary. Possible answers: How deep is the Great Barrier Reef? How extensively has it been explored? What is the most abundant species living there?
2. Answers will vary. Possible answer: Sharks probably live in the Great Barrier Reef; a book about shark habitats would confirm this.

3. B
4. Answers will vary. Students should provide evidence supporting or disproving one of the ideas they generated for questions 1 and 2.

Page 32
1–3. Students' answers will vary. Students should list the type of resource they used and where it was found.
4. Students' topics and sources will vary. Students should find three different sources of information for their topic.

Page 33 Mini-Test 3
1. Answers will vary, but students should be wary of accepting such a controversial theory based on just one person's opinion, no matter how well-respected.
2. Answers will vary, but students should understand that PowerCo's former president has a vested interest in claiming to be innocent. The magazine reporters are probably more objective in evaluating the situation.
3. Answers will vary, but students should conclude that most new immigrants in the late 1800s and

early 1900s chose to live in urban areas instead of rural areas so that they could get jobs in factories and mines. Students should name one source, such as a book on that time period in U.S. history, to confirm their hypothesis.

4. B

Page 34
1. B
2. H
3. Students' answers will vary. Students should describe one creation story they have heard and contrast it with the Tuskegee story.

Page 35
Students' critiques will vary. Students should evaluate their partners' reports using the steps given in the directions.

Page 36
1. A
2. G
3. A
4. G
5. C
6. J
7. Students' paragraphs should give convincing arguments about making a class outing to a local amusement park.

Page 37 Mini-Test 4
1. B
2. J
3. B
4. H
5. D

6. Students' paragraphs should provide convincing reasons to volunteer.

Pages 40–42 Final English Language Arts Test
1. A
2. J
3. D
4. G
5. A
6. G
7. A
8. J
9. D
10. J
11. B
12. J
13. B
14. H
15. D
16. G
17. A
18. G
19. D
20. G

Page 45
1. 21, 23, 25
2. 0, 3, 6, 9, 12, 15
3. 3, 9, 15, 21, 27, 33
4. $y = x + 4$
5. $y = 4x$
6. $y = x - 2$

Page 46
1. B
2. H
3. D
4. J
5. B
6. F

Page 47
1. B
2. H
3. D
4. H
5. Y
6. N
7. Y
8. Y
9. N

10. -7
11. $+15$
12. $\times 3$
13. $\div 7$
14. -6
15. $\div 9$

Page 48
1. $\frac{8}{21}$
2. $\frac{5}{48}$
3. $\frac{3}{10}$
4. $8\frac{2}{3}$
5. $7\frac{1}{12}$
6. $23\frac{4}{5}$
7. $32\frac{1}{2}$
8. $25\frac{17}{32}$
9. $4\frac{1}{2}$
10. 2
11. $\frac{1}{12}$
12. 0
13. $\frac{2}{15}$
14. $4\frac{1}{2}$
15. $17\frac{3}{5}$
16. $\frac{1}{4}$
17. $\frac{5}{7}$
18. $4\frac{1}{2}$

Page 49
1. Y
2. N
3. N
4. Y
5. N
6. Y
7. N
8. N

Page 50
1. T
2. F
3. T
4. T
5. F
6. F
7. T
8. F
9. T
10. T
11. F
12. T
13. T
14. T
15. T
16. <
17. <
18. >
19. =
20. <
21. >
22. >
23. >
24. =
25. >
26. =
27. >
28. <
29. =
30. <
31. >

Page 51
1. 1
2. 2
3. 6
4. 4
5. -4
6. 4
7. 12
8. -7
9. 5
10. 160
11. -9
12. -6

Page 52
1. D
2. H
3. A
4. G
5. C
6. F
7. A

Page 53

1.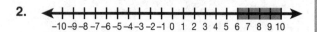

2.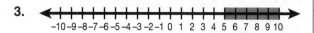

3.

4.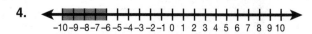

5.

Page 54

1.

x	−3	−2	−1	0	1	2	3
y	−7	−4	−1	2	5	8	11

2.

x	−3	−2	−1	0	1	2	3
y	−6	−4	−2	0	2	4	6

3.

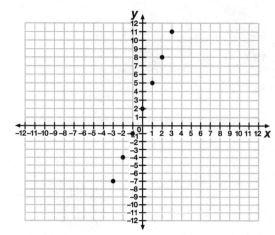

4.

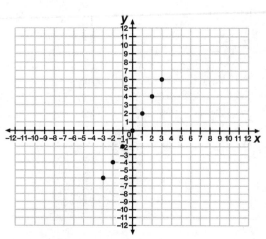

Page 55 Mini-Test 1

1. C
2. F
3. D
4. F
5. B
6. H
7. A
8. F

Page 56

Quadrilateral: 4, 2, 2, 360°

Pentagon: 5, 5, 3, 540°

Hexagon: 6, 9, 4, 720°

Heptagon: 7, 14, 5, 900°

Octagon: 8, 20, 6, 1,080°

Nonagon: 9, 27, 7, 1,260°

Decagon: 10, 35, 8, 1,440°

Dodecagon: 12, 54, 10, 1,800°

Page 57

1. right: 60°
2. obtuse: 110°
3. obtuse: 20°
4. acute: 36°
5. acute: 30°
6. acute 50°
7. right: 50°
8. acute: 71°

Page 58

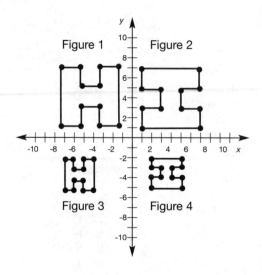

Page 59

1. Reflection across y-axis
2. Translation 8 units left and 2 units down
3. Reflection across y-axis
4. Reflection across x-axis
5. Translation 6 units right and 8 units down
6. Translation 3 units down

Page 60

1.

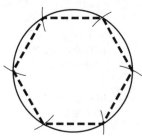

2.

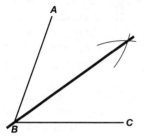

3.

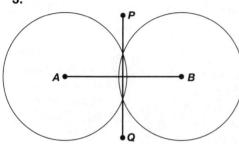

4.

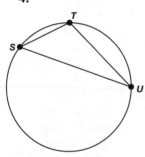

Page 61
1. 1,600 mL
2. 1.621 hL
3. 890 dL
4. 16,000,000 mL
5. 0.09 hL
6. 168,000 cL
7. 6,000 mL
8. 8 cL
9. 60 cL
10. <
11. >
12. =

Page 62
1. 72,000 dg
2. 11,010 mg
3. 1,601.3 dag
4. 6.2 cg
5. 31,000 g
6. 0.0000013 hg

Page 62 continued
7. 0.219 kg
8. 0.0121 dg
9. 11,610 dg
10. >
11. =
12. <

Page 63
1. C
2. G
3. A
4. F
5. D
6. H
7. C
8. H

Page 64
1. A
2. H
3. D
4. G
5. A

Page 65 Mini-Test 2
1. C
2. G
3. D
4. J
5. C
6. G
7. B

Page 66
1. B
2. F
3. B
4. H
5. D
6. J

Page 67
1. C
2. G
3. A
4. F
5. A
6. J
7. B
8. H

Page 68
1. It is likely that about 225 students will order spaghetti.
2. This is a good sample because it is random and it is large enough to represent the entire population.
3. You might use a sample because it can be done more quickly than surveying the entire population.
4. Yes, this sample should be larger than 2% of the population.
5. It is estimated that about 36,400 people voted.
6. No, the poll was not useful because it did not come close to predicting the actual outcome.
7. The poll could have been off because the sample was not random or large enough.

Page 69
1. A
2. F
3. B
4. H
5.

ham — white, wheat, rye
beef — white, wheat, rye
turkey — white, wheat, rye
bologna — white, wheat, rye

6.

black — leather, fabric
red — leather, fabric
tan — leather, fabric

Page 70
1. C
2. H
3. D
4. F
5. D
6. H

Page 71
1. B
2. G
3. B
4. F
5. B
6. H
7. A

Page 72
1. C
2. G
3. B
4. F

Page 73
1. C
2. H
3. A
4. J
5. B
6. G
7. C

Page 74 Mini-Test 3
1. A
2. G
3. A
4. H
5. B
6. G
7. B

Pages 76–78 Final Mathematics Test
1. B
2. J
3. C
4. F
5. C
6. J
7. C
8. H
9. B
10. H
11. C
12. G
13. B
14. H
15. D
16. H
17. B
18. G
19. B
20. G
21. D
22. G
23. C
24. G
25. D
26. F
27. B
28. G

Page 81
1–2. Students' answers will vary. For each pair, students should write a brief report that includes the three parts given in the instructions.

Page 82
1. He asked Josh to be his partner because Josh was a good student.
2. Josh might think that the narrator is trying to prove that he is not prejudiced by asking a black student to be his partner.
3. Josh might want to work by himself, or he might prefer a different partner.
4. Answers will vary but should center on issues of racism and the difficulty people of different races often have in discussing racial issues with one another.

Page 83
1. Items such as nuts, wood, corn shucks, cane, apples, and gourds were used to make toys.
2. Sunday is the day of worship for Christians. Many devout Christians of the Old South refrained from work and all secular pursuits on Sunday and required their children to do the same.
3. Students' answers will vary but should focus on activities such as hunting, farming, chopping wood, working with tools such as saws, etc. These activities are reflected in the kinds of toys children played with.
4. Students' answers will vary. Possible answer: Children's toys often reflect adult activities and what is important to adults. Today's parents often give their children electronic or computer toys, reflecting the importance of computers in today's world.

Page 84
1. B
2. H
3. A

Page 85
1. C
2. F
3. B

Page 86
1. C
2. G
3. A
4. The population density in the area surrounding Oslo is probably greater than the density in the area surrounding Tromsø because the climate is much more hospitable in the vicinity of Oslo.

Page 87
1. B
2. J
3. C
4. H

Page 88 Mini-Test 1
1. the death of Marcus Aurelius in A.D. 180.
2. Students' answers will vary. Possible answer: Although the *Pax Romana* was beneficial to much of Rome, many people were enslaved during the period. Even in Rome, not everyone enjoyed the prosperity of the age. Therefore, the era cannot be considered the greatest of all.
3. Students' answers will vary. One possible answer: The founding brothers have a god for a parent. The Romans would want to show that Rome was divinely established and was therefore superior and "deserved" to rule the world.
4. D

Page 89
1. N
2. S
3. S
4. N
5. S
6. S
7. N
8. S
9. N
10. S
11. These ads seem to suggest that mothers do all the housework and cooking, and really enjoy this.

12. These ads suggest that girls are more vain and care more about their appearance than boys do.
13. These ads suggest that boys are rough-and-tumble and enjoy these toys more than girls do.

Page 90
1. genetics and relationships with peers
2. She supported her theory with studies of adopted children, as well as other studies that showed that children are more likely to imitate the behavior of their friends and schoolmates than the behavior of their parents.
3. No, these studies do not support her theory, because they show that how parents raise their children does have a strong impact on the children's development.
4. Students' answers will vary but should include two examples to support their answers.

Page 91
1. A
2. G
3. Students' answers will vary. Possible response: Married couples sometimes get a break on their taxes.
4. Students' answers will vary. Possible response: legal costs for divorces are expensive.
5. Today, most Americans are in their late 20s when they marry for the first time. In the 1960s, they tended to marry for the first time in their early 20s. Students' answers will vary regarding reasons for this. Possible response: Women are more economically independent now than 40–50 years ago and feel less of a need to marry soon after high school.

Page 92
1. C
2. G
3. Prohibition was repealed in 1933. Many students will answer that alcohol-related crime (e.g., bootlegging) increased dramatically during Prohibition, resulting in the call for repeal, or that outlawing alcohol was simply impractical. Other answers may also be acceptable.
4. Students' answers will vary. Possible response: Churches and religious groups usually have more influence in "dry" counties than in "wet" counties. Dry areas are especially prominent in the South and Midwest, the so-called "Bible Belt," where religion has more of an influence on society than elsewhere in the country.
5. Students' answers will vary but should indicate what the group did and what motivated them.

Page 93 Mini-Test 2
1. B
2. F
3. Students' answers will vary, but students should explain their answers.
4. Students' answers will vary.
5. Possible responses— Family: take care of sick family members; Marriage: be faithful to your spouse; Religion: pray regularly; Schools: do not cheat on tests.

Page 94
1. B
2. H
3. A
4. G
5. Students' answers will vary but might focus on the importance of citizens knowing what their government is doing and voting responsibly.

Page 95
1. D
2. J
3. C
4. J
5. A
6. F
7–10. Students should name the current president, current chief justice of the Supreme Court, current congressional representative from their district, and one current senator from their state.

President—executive; chief justice—judicial; representative and senator—legislative

Page 96
1. A
2. J
3. A
4. G
5. A
6. J
7. Answers will vary. Most students will conclude that people wanted to purchase the generators because they needed another source for their electricity. They were willing to pay a higher price since their normal source of electricity was unavailable.

Page 97
1. C
2. G
3. B
4. J

Page 98
1. D
2. J
3. A
4. G
5. A

Page 99
1. The regulations indicate that Americans during the Depression placed a high value on morality and respect for religion.
2. The regulations show that there was a concern that motion pictures did not always uphold the moral values of the time and might encourage negative behaviors.

Page 100 Mini-Test 3
1. A
2. G
3. D
4. H
5. B
6. J
7. Students' answers will vary. Possible answer: The Internet makes it possible to transmit music and video images easily and at no charge. The music and film industry has lobbied for laws restricting such behavior.

Page 101
1. B
2. H
3. D
4. J

Page 102
1. A
2. J
3. A
4. H
5. C
6. G
7. B
8. G

Page 103
Students' are to write a letter to the editor of the local newspaper, following the guidelines given in the activity.

Page 104
1. C
2. G
3. D
4. G
5. A
6. Students' answers will vary. Many students will perceive such a law as a great imposition on their freedom.

Page 105 Mini-Test 4
1. A
2. H
3. B
4. J
5. C
6. J
7. B

Pages 108–110 Final Social Studies Test
1. A
2. J
3. B
4. H
5. C
6. J
7. C
8. H
9. C
10. F
11. B
12. G
13. C
14. J
15. D
16. H
17. D
18. F
19. C

Page 114
1. A
2. J
3. C
4. G

Page 115
1. S
2. S
3. N
4. S
5. S
6. S
7. S
8. N
9. S
10. S
11. S
12. S
13. S
14. S
15. S
16. S
17. S
18. Students should describe how the wheels, axles, bearings, board, and other associated parts of a skateboard function together.

Page 116
1. C
2. G
3. A
4. J
5. B
6. J
7. D

Page 117
1. B
2. H
3. Answers will vary. Possible answer: Lauren made accurate, detailed records of her experiment.
4. Answers will vary. Possible answer: Lauren should have either used new flashlights for both experiments or used the same old flashlights for both experiments. This would have given her a clearer idea of how long the batteries last under specific conditions.

Page 118 Mini-Test 1
1. C
2. F
3. A
4. G
5. B
6. H
7. Answers will vary but should demonstrate that the student understands that similar scientific investigations seldom produce exactly the same results.

Page 119
1. A
2. G
3. A
4. H
5. B

Page 120
1. A
2. H
3. A
4. J
5. C
6. G
7. A

Page 121
1. mixture
2. compound
3. compound
4. mixture
5. solution
6. compound
7. element

8. element
9. mixture
10. solution
11. B
12. F
13. A compound consists of atoms of two or more different elements bound together *chemically;* a mixture or solution consists of two or more different elements and/or compounds *physically* intermingled.

Pages 122–123
1. B
2. H
3. A
4. H
5. B
6. H
7. D
8. F
9. B
10. F

Pages 124–125
1. C
2. G
3. B
4. G
5. D
6. J
7. A
8. G
9. A

Page 126
1. B
2. H
3. B
4. H
5. A
6. F

Page 127 Mini-Test 2
1. B
2. F
3. D
4. G
5. B
6. H

Page 128
1–4. Students' responses will vary, but they should accurately complete each table.
5. Answers will vary, but students should describe both the intended and unintended consequences of the invention.

Page 129
1. D
2. G
3. D
4. F
5. B (1.5–4 gallons)
6. E (2–5 gallons)
7. D (8–15 gallons)
8. A (17–24 gallons)
9. C (50 gallons)
10. Answers will vary, but students should list all of their activities that used water and estimate the amount of water used.
11. Students' ideas for saving water will vary. Possible ideas: Wait until there's a full load before running the washer or dishwasher; take shorter showers; turn off the water while brushing teeth or washing hands.

Page 130
1. D
2. G
3. B
4. H
5. D

Page 131 Mini-Test 3
1. B
2. J
3. D
4. H
5. D
6. Answers will vary, but students should list one invention for each area, as well as the inventor and his or her nationality.

Pages 133–135
Final Science Test
1. B
2. F
3. A
4. J
5. C
6. F
7. C
8. G
9. B
10. H
11. D
12. G
13. B
14. J
15. A
16. H
17. C
18. F
19. A
20. J

NOTES

NOTES

NOTES

NOTES

NOTES